The *Keepers* of the *Sand*
A Waikiki Beachboy's Story

Barry Napoleon

The Keepers of the Sand: A Waikiki Beachboy's Story by Barry Napoleon
Copyright © 2017 by Barry Napoleon

Cover and Book Design Copyright © 2017 by Shawn Young

All rights reserved. No part of this publication may be reproduced or transmitted in any form or by any means, electronic or mechanical, including photocopying, recording, or any information storage and retrieval system, without the prior written permission of the publishers and respective copyright holders, except for in the case of brief quotations embodied in critical articles and reviews.

For more information, visit www.barrynapoleon.com

Front and back cover photographs by Clarence Maki

ISBN: 978-0-692-87213-0 (paperback)

First Edition (July 2017)
Printed in the United States of America

Contents

Introduction 1
The Keepers of the Sand 5
Epilogue 327
Acknowledgements 329

*A very special thank you to
Valentina Tondaleiya Lopez-Cannon
whose generous support made
the publication of this book possible.*

What would you have me do?
Seek for the patronage of some great man,
And like a creeping vine on a tall tree
Crawl upward, where I can not stand alone?
No, thank you!
    Be a buffoon in the vile hope of teasing
    Out a smile on some cold face?
    No, thank you!
I am too proud to be a parasite,
And if my nature wants the germ that grows
Towering to heven like the mountain pine,
Or like the oak, sheltering multitudes –
I stand, not high, it may be –
But alone!

Edmond Rostrand
Cyrano de Bergerac

Dear Reader:

This is the story of my island as I have known it. It is my story and a people's story. Good times, bad times, proud times, and not so very proud times. I have not white-washed one word.

It may well be that you will uncover a bit of your own past buried somewhere in these pages, for much of this story evolves from you. No *pilikia*. Real names were written in the sand and washed clean by the next high tide. That's the Hawaiian way.

Aloha,
Barry Napoleon

Introduction

I suppose there are a lot of reasons why a person wants to write a book. Mine is very simple: I do what I have to do. It is not in the quest of fame and fortune; hell, I've been around enough to know these two elusive characters all too well! The odds for their attainment are horrendous. I'm not sure I would know what to do with them if I caught them. I'm not even sure I want to chase after them. I'm a good provider. I love my life and those who are dear to me. No, that's not what I'm seeking.

My reason for making this attempt is a burning desire to share. In Hawaii, we call this the spirit of *Aloha*. The feeling became so intense that I had no alternative but to plan in and take on what was, for me, a task of monumental proportion. Bit that in itself is an expression of this spirit of *aloha* which, in turn, is the driving force behind this book.

Blackout! Whoever heard of a goodwill ambassador named Blackout? Or Jewjaw? Or Buckshot? Or Apple? Yet names like these have been carried back to countries all over the world. How many countless tourists have left a part of their lives in Hawaii in the care of a Blue Makua or a Zulu or a Rabbit? How many memories still linger amongst kindred should enduring freezing temperatures in far-off places because of Bobby Krewson, Buddy Kahanamoku, and Mud Warner? Guys like these have been written up or done famous deeds. They have existed by dealing with thousands of people every year, sharing their island with them, and giving of their *aloha* spirit. They would work all day in the sun, and play with visitors all night. When it was time to leave, they bought leis and escorted their new friends to the boats and to the planes, accepting a 'Thank you, Dukie,' 'see you next time, Jama.' 'I'll never forget you, Lloyd Kellet' as payment in full. Where else in the world, in what part of time, would a guy take time off from his work to run downtown to the likes of Maunakea Street and buy *manapua* so that some guy could taste it and pay him with a smile? Watanabe's done this. So has Alex. And so have we all. I'd like to have a nickel for every box of home-grown mangoes Bobby Ah Choy, Cluny, Menehune, or Moku brought down to the beach for tourists, saying, "*Hele mai kau kau.*" ("Come, eat.")

They're gone from the beach now, a lot of the boys—Bobby Ah Choy, Don Ho, Joe Bailey, Steamboat. *Mahalo* for the help, brother. And *mahalo* to the older guys that showed us the way. Kalakaua, Panama Dave, Chick Daniels, Turkey Love, and Sammy Amalu. As kids, we would hang around the beach, Samson, Nigger Dan, Georgie, Buster, Jesse, watching Steamboat and Splash Lyons take another canoe full of tourists out into the surf off Waikiki. Woodie Brown at the helm of his flying catamaran taught us more about winds and currents than any textbook could possibly convey. Just ask Leroy Ah Choy, he'll show you.

The Kahanamoku Brothers—Duke, Sergeant, Sam, and

Louie—stood so tall and proud as we watched the waves thunder in from Steamer Lane. They are what surfing and Hawaii is all about. And they were our teachers. Aloha spirit is made by the people: Emma and Alice at the lei stands, the fresh scent of ginger in the air; Webley Edwards and Al Kealoha Perry making music behind Alfred Alpaka; George Wainapau and Haunani Kahalawai bringing to the mainland the sounds of Waikiki as *Hawaii Calls* radio show.

Yes, the Spirit of *Aloha* is still in the air and, God willing, I hope I can give it to you.

Chapter 1

Hawaii was the last group of Polynesian islands to be settled. Migrations from Tahiti began arriving in the 5th century. Each island was ruled by a chief. If the island was large, one might find several chiefs, each responsible for his own territory. Chiefs were believed to be direct descendants of the gods. Rigid class distinctions were observed and the Chief's powers were absolute. There were no acts of cruelty or injustice, but they exercised their authority in a regal and impressive manner. Captain Cook's logs tell of a young chief dealing with a dissenter by picking him up and tossing him off the ship into the sea.

At the time of Captain Cook, in 1776, the Hawaiian Islands were divided into four kingdoms. The island of Hawaii was the largest, and was under the rule of Kalaniopuu, who also had holdings on Maui. He visualized all islands united under one rule. This ambition was realized by his nephew, Kamehameha, the founder of a dynasty that continued governing in direct descent until 1893. A bloodless revolution established a republic that transferred its sovereignty to the United States in 1898. In 1959, Hawaii was admitted as the 50th state.

Old Hawaiians would say that Oahu is the navel of the world. The exact center of that navel, then, would be Honolulu, for some 3.2 million tourists pass through every year. It was here that David Kalakaua ruled his people from the glittering throne room in the Iolani Palace. Today, Kalakaua Avenue is the main artery of Waikiki, the most famous beach in the world. The domain is small now—a thin band of glistening sand reduced even further, at times, deeding on the whims of the tides—but it is still the territory of the sons of Kalakaua.

Chapter 2

Last night's high tide had swept the beach clean of all traces of yesterday. The canoes were lined up and the rental boards were standing on edge in the soft sand. I was seated behind a plywood stand supported by 2x4s and covered over with a thatched roof to protect me from the sun's harsh rays. Pictures of good-looking past visitors were proudly displayed under a thin layer of fiberglass that covers the counter of my desk (an old wooden table with an umbrella through the center) where I marked the sea and air conditions on a small green clipboard.

"Hey, boy, what do you get for a ride in one of those canoes?"

My eyes worked from the bottom up: white sneakers, black socks pulled tightly to mid-calf, heavy chalk white thighs covered with stringy black hair. An expensive cigar was wedged between the fingers of a hand attached to a wrist by a gold ID bracelet. The matching trunks and aloha shirt did little to liven up a featureless face, half hidden under a golf cap sporting some home club crest.

"The canoe ride. How much do you charge?"

"Three fifty."

"I got the wife and two kids over there. How about two bucks? We're guests of the hotel."

"Surf is no good. Bad day for canoes."

"You an employee of this hotel?"

"No."

"Well, you work here, don't you?"

"Yes."

"What's your name?"

"Napoleon."

I return to my clip board. He studies me a moment. I could imagine him wondering, *Is this island relaxation? Insolence? Both?*

I glanced up. He turned and moved unsteadily through the sand towards the rows of backrests.

"Hey, honey! That guy told me his name is Napoleon."

"Napoleon? That's a funny name for a Hey-waa-yan."

Chapter 3

The Grand Ballroom at the Palais Royal was alive with gaiety. French dignitaries and their ladies, highly perfumed and attired in splendid regalia, twirled over the marble floor to music played by the finest musicians the court could provide. The Napoleonic Empire was on the threshold of its most brilliant and imposing form.

The receiving line seemed endless. The Emperor Napoleon struck a dashing figure. He wore his vanity with all the modesty of a resplendent peacock in repose. The adulations and well wishes heaped upon the members of the Royal Family were being savored by all but one of the recipients.

Napoleon's younger brother, Louis, was a study in preoccupation. Compliments fell on deaf ears and his eyes darted back and forth as if looking for something he knew wasn't there. Louis needed a way out. An excuse to leave this boring circus. He had more exciting affairs to attend to.

Earlier that week, while exercising his horse down by the River Seine, he had happened upon the most exciting woman he had ever seen in his life. A group of young girls had gathered along the bank. They giggled shyly and turned away as the handsome uniformed rider approached. · All but one, and she stood out like a wild orchid in a field of daisies. Her skin was golden bronze and her hair as black as ebony. The girl's piercing brown eyes met his in direct confrontation, causing an explosion of adrenalin to go racing through his body.

It was not hard for a man of his royal stature to discreetly discover all there was to know about this brown skinned apparition. Her name was Tiare (the Tahitian for a type of Gardenia flower). She was the daughter of Pōmare II, the native chief of Tahiti, a French possession in the far-off Pacific. She had been sent to France for formal schooling. Information of this kind only served to feed the flame already ablaze in the loins of this hot-blooded, rapacious Frenchman. He rode through the park on several different occasions that week, three times coming upon this same group of girls. All three times, the eyes were there, each silent encounter reinforcing the bond growing between them.

When Tiare returned to her room that Saturday after the evening meal, she noticed a sealed envelope placed innocently on the small table next to her bed. She opened it and stood next to the window to take full advantage of the last vestige of daylight now turned a brilliant pink over the city of Paris.

"Tonight, when the tower strikes ten at the bridge by the Seine, the rider on horseback wants to see you again. He knows all about you and where you are from. Let this be our secret. Hope you will come."

She smiled at the obvious attempt of poetic self-effacement should the note stray and fall into the wrong hands. She had done a bit of investigating on her own and was fully aware of the author's true identity and the risks involved in accepting such an invitation. But her free Tahitian spirit, so long pent up conforming to the rigors and restrictions of this new academic life, soared at the thought of a secret rendezvous in the dark with such a handsome young man. In fact, she had harbored such fanciful ideas since the first day she saw him, but felt herself powerless to pursue them. In France, young ladies did not wear flowers in their hair, and back home a girl would not wear a heavy long dress and layers of restrictive petticoats over a body lean and hard and as capable as any man's of scaling walls, bounding unseen through bushes and across streams. From the bottom of her dresser drawer, almost secreted away, she removed a pareau and kicked off her shoes.

At the ball, Louis was suddenly overcome with severe lower abdominal pains. His condition was at once the cause of great concern, but he assured one and all that what he needed most of all was a chamber pot, a little seclusion, and a night's rest. The evening's excitement had been too much for him, overwrought as he was with matters of international consequence. With that, he excused himself and, walking with a slight stoop, headed for the commode. Once outside the Palais Royale, Louis made a miraculous recovery. He hurried across the courtyard and out onto the Rue de la Rivoli, doubling back, cautiously working the shadows.

Confident that his movements had not been observed, he entered the park as Notre Dame began to toll the hour. Paris after dark was not the safest place to be. Thieves and city toughs roamed about. But for Louis, the quest far outweighed the risk.

Rumors of forbidden pleasure awaiting those who ventured

to the South Seas were running rampant throughout France. Crews from the great sailing ships could talk of little else upon their return. The tales were outlandish, almost unbelievable. But Louis had read the ship's log from Bouganville's last voyage himself. Could changes in latitude make the difference? Were these people from *Otahiti* more animal than human? Still, he had never seen such beauty in a woman in his entire life. If she were part animal, then humans should be so beautiful. Except for her dark coloring, she appeared as normal as the other girls. Her records showed no devious behavior. He'd heard of their pagan gods and rituals and yet, according to the information he had received, her religious deportment was above reproach.

The muffled rhetorical meanderings of a mild-mannered ship's cook, answering to charges of desertion, kept re-entering his mind. He had told the Tribunal of being forcibly detained and stripped naked by a band of native girls. One by one they took turns indulging themselves in all manner of sexual activity. True or not, the poor fellow was found in such a weakened state that for a time the ship's doctor feared for his life.

The sound of rushing water brought his own situation to mind. The sudden onset of a nervous quiver turned his stealthy gait into the loose-jointed shuffle of a stringed puppet. A low hanging branch caught the bridge of his nose, extended out and snapped back, knocking the plumed hat from his head. An instinctive defensive reaction went awry, he let out a cry of alarm and tumbled head over heels down the embankment.

Tiare had arrived at the bridge early. It was quite dark and she did not relish the idea of standing alone, exposed to the whims of any passerby. She made her way down the bank to the security of the flowing water and waited. Time passed slowly and the seeds of discretion began to grow in her mind. She was, after all, a guest in a strange land. What did she know of the man's true intentions? And to come dressed in this manner! Would he think she had taken leave of her senses? Had she?

She heard the cry and watched the fall. It was not a great fall, really, and his recovery was so rapid that her momentary alarm turned to amusement at so pretentious a figure floundering in the dark waters for a silly hat floating impishly away. Laughter is a universal language.

Laughter shared is the common denominator of understanding. It releases tensions and soothes the soul. Hers proved infectious. The distance between them closed and they shared an embrace of lovers long parted. With a single movement of her right hand, the tapa pareau, as soft as gauze, parted and slipped to the ground. Her left hand then groped for the combination to the most ridiculous make of trousers she had ever tried to open in her life.

That warm summer Parisian night and for a good many nights thereafter, royal Napoleonic juices blended with those from a long line of Tahitian kings and queens to the pulsating rhythms of a Tamure and the slow deliberate beats of a Minuet. The result of such a union was inevitable. The attitudes concerning the result were, however, worlds apart.

In Tahiti, as in all the islands of the South Pacific, children were a welcome commodity. Anybody's, any time. If a child of questionable origin happened along—and there must have been quite a few—it was taken in by a family to be loved and raised as their own. Illegitimacy, though rampant in Europe, was cause for grave concern, even shame. This was particularly evident among members of the upper social sphere. A baby with a different skin color would be intolerable. A general solution was infanticide. Thus, as her condition became more and more apparent, so did Louis' intentions for solving his crisis. Tiare had her own answer. Very quietly and with great dignity, she caught the next boat for home.

It is not unusual for Tahitians to change their names as a result of any incident or phenomenon which catches their fancy. King Tu of Tahiti adopted the name of Pomare, which means Night Cough. Having spent a night sleeping out in the mountains, he developed a cough which one of his attendants referred to as a night cough. This struck his fancy and it is the name by which he and his descendants are known. His son, Põmare II, succeeded his father. He became one of the first Polynesian converts to Christianity and a victim of the missionaries' zeal. Põmare II died a recluse on the small island of Motu Uta in the middle of Papeete Harbor, with a bible in one hand and a bottle in the other.

Napoleon? Sure, that's a funny name for a Hawaiian. But so is Night Cough.

Chapter 4

Rain beat down on a corrugated tin roof, then stopped as quickly as it began. Trade wind clouds, relieved of their burdens of moisture, sailed away to the accompaniment of palm fronds clapping in the breeze. Somewhere, a coconut took leave of its cluster and plummeted to the ground, landing with a dull thud in the thick pili grass. A full moon peered in through the window at a small boy laying wide-eyed in bed.

He listened as water continued to drip from the eaves and watched tiny crystal rivulets chase one another down the illuminated pane of glass. Eyelids grew heavy with dreams of the marvelous things tomorrow would bring.

With the first light of dawn, shreds of clouds began to gather up on Mt. Tantalus. The boy knew the signs. The trade winds would blow and that would be good for the waves.

If there were waves, that is. With an excitement only youth seems able to generate, he pedaled his bicycle like a madman down the narrow street, over dirt paths, through puddles, past the swamp, on and on toward the sea wall at Waikiki. Today, hopefully, he would be the first to know. Then he could race back home and awaken his older brothers with the news, "Hey! Waikiki got big wave!"

On that day, the surf line was just coming into view when he heard the dull explosions and saw the sky turn black over Pearl Harbor.

Chapter 5

My father had the equivalent of a sixth grade education from the public school system and a masters degree from the school of life. Formal education, however, became a prerequisite in his mind where his children were concerned. In order to afford us the opportunities for the schooling he never had, he worked very hard. An electrician by trade, he supplemented the lean periods by working as a butcher and a cow-puncher. He served the City and County of Honolulu for 20 years as Captain of the Life Guards. He was as just as he was strict. I never met a man who tried so hard to be perfect.

In Honolulu in 1939, there were two types of schools: the English standard school for the Haoles and the common public school for the locals. If your father happened to be one of the High Mucky Mucks and you didn't speak like a Hawaiian, you could get into the English standard school. On the other hand, if you did not speak like a *haole*, they sent you to the public school with all the *Kanakas*. The seeds of hostility could not have been planted in a more fertile environment.

Consider the rationale of impetuous youth. I'm a Kanaka and all my friends are Kanakas. This was originally our land. I'll speak like a Kanaka and go to the Kanaka school. Let the *haoles* do their own thing.

My mother is Japanese and the Japanese are stoic, strong, proud and quietly ambitious. I still remember her words, drilled into me over and over again: "Try and better yourself;" "speak like a *haole*;" "act like a *haole*;" "you're just as good as the *haoles*;" "you are going to have to learn to get along in a *haole* world, my son, or the world will pass you by." This constant reminder planted the seed of doubt in my mind.

Money was always a problem and landlords were quick with the solution: pay up or move. As a result, I went to six different schools my first seven years. In the 7th grade, I played hooky for half the school year. Each morning, my father would give me $0.20: $0.15 for lunch and $0.05 for milk. I would show up at school one half hour early and head for the boys' room. There was always a crap game going on. If I lost, I'd borrow money from a winner, promising him I'd repay the next day.

The world's gonna pass me by? Huh! The world should have it so good. I would go up into the mountains. There were good things to eat in the mountains. Crawfish, fresh fruit, and clear clean water. I didn't even have to worry about snakes. The mongooses had taken care of that problem long ago. When the rains came, the ti leaf slides were fast and exciting. And there was the beach. Always the beach and the ocean. Then, one day my father paid a visit to the school. He went right to the principal.

"Hey, what kind of school are you running here? How come

you don't send me any reports on how my son is doin'?"

"I'm sorry, sir. Who is your son?"

"Barry. Barry Napoleon."

"Mr. Napoleon, we don't have Barry on our rolls this year. We thought you had moved!"

• • •

Bang!

My father always hit first and explained afterwards.

"You know what I hit you for?"

"No."

"You haven't been goin' to school! That's what I hit you for. You want to grow up to be a nobody?"

The following day, I was back in school and spent weekends under my father's watchful eye. As Captain of the Life Guards, he found all kinds of things for me to do. I was always big for my age and had now become a powerful swimmer. My father was still upset over the school incident, but I could detect a glint of pride in his eye over my prowess in the ocean. Holding my breath under water was my specialty. I inherited that ability from my father, who could stay under for well over three minutes.

One night we were eating dinner and there was a knock at the door. A small Japanese fisherman stood on the porch oblivious to the flying termites buzzing around his distraught face.

"Captain Napoleon lives here?"

"Yeah, just a minute. Hey, Dad! It's for you!"

I couldn't bring myself to leave this pathetic looking figure alone, so I waited for my father to approach. The fisherman told us of losing his young son to the ocean earlier that day. The boy had been swept off a rock by a wave and sucked under the sea. It's a common story in the Islands.

White markers commemorating those lost at sea are everywhere. The Japanese have this thing about their dead.

"The Fire Department has been unable to help us locate his body," he said. "They say he will never be found. Captain Napoleon, find him. Please, don't let my son stay in the water all night. Please, my wife…"

His voice trailed off.

The little man, termites clinging to his clothes, grew filmy in front of me. I blinked my eyes and wiped a tear from my cheek. I turned and walked into the kitchen.

My father and I followed the little man to the beach. Captain Napoleon issued his orders. We were to remain where we were until he told us otherwise. He pulled off his clothes and plunged into the waves. Once outside the surfline he rolled over on his back and began to float. For three hours, he remained as motionless as flotsam. The ocean drift carried him far down the shoreline. We kept a silent vigil, not exchanging one word. I spotted movement in the water, a sudden surge of currents. Dad was in the riptide and moving rapidly out to sea. He began to wave his arms. I ran down the beach, climbed up some lava rocks and dove in. I went with the rip, swimming as hard as I could. I looked up and my father was treading water just outside the riptide's borders. He motioned me to follow him down. We made a deep dive.

The boy's body was stuck in a crevice in the reef. Dad moved his foot and we brought him to the surface. It was my first encounter with death.

Chapter 6

My father was superintendent of the War Memorial Natatorium. It is situated on the water at the foot of Diamond Head, overlooking Waikiki. This outdoor swim stadium feeds and filters itself by means of large pipes that extend out into the ocean. My dad and I were standing by the concrete ledge that acts as a buffer between the pool and the sea. The tide was high, sending walls of water into the air with each in-coming swell.

From one end of the pool, we heard a kid yell, "Help! Help! My friend is stuck in the pipe!" We ran over to the frightened boy. "He dove off the ledge and didn't come up!"

The only thing rising to the surface was the tell-tale bubbling from the pipes. My father nudged me on the shoulder and we hit the water together. The ocean's surge pushed off the sea wall, creating a backwash that rendered us as helpless as two bobbing corks. The natatorium seemed to pull away from us. The ominous pipe, two and a half feet in diameter and fifteen feet long, was sucking water like a killer whale.

"I'm going down to the pipes," he said. "Give me a ten count and you follow. When you see me go in, surface. Take in as much air as you can and come down after me. I can't swim out of that thing backwards. You're gonna have to reach in and pull me out!"

He disappeared beneath the water like a startled seal. I rose with the incoming tidal surge and before it slapped into the wall, I too was gone. I saw my father enter the pipe, followed by a stream of silver bubbles. I swam to the surface and expelled all the air from my lungs. I inhaled deeply and dove down. With my lungs already on the verge of bursting, I called on every ounce of reserve I had. Dad had the kid in his hands when I pulled him back out of the pipe. He brought the boy to the surface and swam with him to the steps. I climbed out quickly and my father handed the almost lifeless body to me.

"Is he dead? Is he dead?" the mother cried.

We were too busy to answer. Working feverishly but methodically, we applied artificial respiration. Seconds later, the boy coughed.

That night, I looked, the word 'hero' up in the dictionary. "In mythology and legend, a man celebrated for his strength and bold exploits."

I really didn't need a dictionary. I knew: my dad was a hero.

Chapter 7

My brothers and sisters were all enrolled in the English standard schools. I began to feel left out. I didn't really want to grow up to be a nobody, particularly not after a whole summer of working alongside my father. I was filled with pride and a sense of accomplishment and I made up my mind that I would take the entrance test and pass it. My sisters worked with me on my English and by the time the examinations came around, I was ready. The results came back with a letter of acceptance into Robert Louis Stevenson, an intermediate English standard school.

Everybody was happy. It was a new beginning, a fresh start. We bought books and new clothes, and I was on my way. It was quite a dramatic change for me. The educational standards were much higher and the teachers demanded strict, attentive behavior. I was in trouble from the very first day, one disciplinary infraction after the other. I was unjustly blamed for an errant fart, pleaded guilty to goosing a girl in the hall, not to mention smoking, hanging a guy by his belt loop on a sewer pipe, punching out a guy in class, and bursting into the girls' lavatory in hot pursuit.

My best subject was art. I excelled in it. Odd that it proved to be the cause of my final downfall at school. I was in the library sketching a typical South Sea Island scene, a waterfall spilling into a lush mountain pool with naked island girls sunning themselves on exposed ledges and rocks. Granted, I was paying close attention to detail where the girls' anatomies were concerned, but nothing to merit the treatment I was about to receive.

My teacher, curious as to what could be holding my attention throughout the entire library period, looked over my shoulder and took this simple drawing as a direct affront to God, women, and her missionary heritage. She grabbed my paper and in the process of yanking me out of my seat tore two buttons off of my new shirt.

"Hey, how come you tore the buttons off my shirts? How would you like me to do that to you?"

I reached up and tore the front of her blouse. My hand got caught in her bra and her boob fell out.

The principal passed sentence on me. Three lessons from from the Board of Education. This was a wooden paddle about three feet long, eight inches wide, and three-quarters of an inch thick, interspersed with holes to cut down air resistance. I was made to bend over a chair while he stepped back, rolled up his sleeves and took aim.

The first blow almost drove me through the wall. The second time he hit me I knew for sure my backside was cut and bleeding. I was about to turn around and take a poke at this guy. I knew, however, if I could endure one more time, that all of this trouble I was in would be over. CRACK! I was in such pain I thought I was going to die. Gritting my teeth, I wiped the sweat from my brow and stood up. My hand was shaking as I put my wallet back in my pants pocket. The man had a weird, orgasmic look on his face. As young as I was, I sensed that there was something more here than just a disciplinary action. I looked him straight in the eye, never shedding a tear, and said, "Is that all you're gonna do?"

His voice took on a higher pitch and his hand began to shake.

"No, young man. That's not all I'm going to do. Get back over that chair. I'm going to give you three more!"

"No, you ain't!"

With that, I punched him in the face, dove out the window, and ran away.

Chapter 8

My great, great, great grandfather on my mother's side was the illegitimate son of Prince Kuhio. When a small child of five or six, he was put on a boat and carried far out to sea. He was thrown into the ocean, a human sacrifice to appease an angry god. While he was floundering in the water, a shark approached and swam alongside him—an *aumakua* (family god). This great fish picked him up and brought him back to shore, so the family legend goes. His royal lineage was not forgotten. When Queen Liliuokalani died, the royal family sent a special emissary in a grand horse and carriage to Pualei Lane, where the old families lived, to escort great grandfather to the funeral.

My grandparents on my father's side owned vast amount of land on the Island of Maui. Up until 1927, the family had been collecting rents from their acreage. The tenants were the sugar people of Pioneer Mill, a subsidiary of American Factors, one of the original Big Five companies.

Suddenly the rental payments stopped. My grandfather was told they would not be resumed until he could show title to this land. This was a part of the great Kanaina Estate.

Charles Kanaina was a brother of King Kamehameha. My grandfather was a legal heir. He sent my father to Kahului on the Island of Maui to get to the bottom of this matter and collect our records. Upon his arrival he was informed that the old courthouse had burned down and all such records had been destroyed in the fire.

My father returned to Honolulu confused and empty-handed. Why hand't the loss of such important information been reported?

Grandfather dispatched him immediately to Kauai. Certainly duplicates or even originals could be found there, in Lihue, the capital. He met with a stone wall. His persistence in the matter resulted in another tale of a mysterious fire.

In 1929 the family scraped together $5,000 and sent my father to San Francisco. He contacted an attorney, Barry Ulrich, who had been highly recommended as an expert in such matters. Ulrich accepted the $5,000 as a retainer and returned to Honolulu with my father to start investigative procedures. My father was so pleased with this man's proclaimed legal stature and professed intentions that when I was born that same year he named me after him.

His reports reaffirming their rightful position were constant and incontrovertible. Not more than a week before the appointed court date, Barry Ulrich disappeared. My father found he had booked passage on the steamship and was somewhere between Honolulu and San Francisco. He had cancelled the court date and dropped our case. Incensed, my grandmother, a practicing kahuna, put a curse on him. Six months later, the news reached us that Barry Ulrich was dead.

From 1929 until the present, this case has been hanging in limbo. No one really owns this land for clear title has never been shown. From time to time proclamations are issued to the Kanaina Estate heirs 'to step forward or forever hold your peace.'

Grandfather would step forward and the sugar people could never claim the land. Packaged with parcels on Oahu, the value today would be somewhere in the neighborhood of fifty million dollars.

Human sacrifices to appease angry gods. Where is my *aumakua?*

Chapter 9

In the forties, my father leased the second floor of a dilapidated downtown building, the Natatorium Athletic Club, the biggest boxing gym in Honolulu. A dark, wooden stairway led fighters, managers, trainers, on-lookers and gamblers off the street and up into the raw, rough world of the prize fighter. Go to any big city in the world, they're all the same, these over-crowded, gamey, smoke-filled places. It has never ceased to amaze me how surroundings of this kind can turn out products able to withstand the rigors and physical demands put upon them to survive in this most violent of all man's so-called sports. I guess you've got to be tough in the first place and then tough breeds tougher. No one leaves the ring unscathed. Carl "BoBo" Olsen, one-time Middle Weight Champion of the World, was a product of our gym.

In addition to running the gym, dad had his own small stable of fighters, mostly amateurs. He was convinced boxing was really the manly art of self-defense, a character builder.

"Get the kids off the streets and into the gym."

Tuesday night was fight night. Smokers, we called them. Television hadn't come to the Islands in those days. The fights were the biggest attraction in town. The crowd had to be the roughest anywhere. Sailors, soldiers, marines, Hawaiians, Samoans, Portuguese, Filipinos, Orientals, all sizes, shapes and ages mixed together. All ready to bet on anything. Sometimes the fights in the stands were better than those up in the ring.

Where the amateurs were concerned, a club would get a percentage of the gate. The size of the percentage was based upon how many fighters you put in the ring. My father's club was in dire need of new equipment. So it was with the betterment of youth in mind when he said to me one hot, humid Sunday morning.

"You see that guy standin' over there?"

"The heavy guy leanin' up against the wall?"

"That's him. Could you give him a lickin'?"

"I don't know maybe . . yeah, I think so."

"Good 'Cuz you're gonna fight him Tuesday night."

I was just seventeen and I'd never done any boxing in the ring before. Just street stuff and I was getting pretty good at that. I had spent countless hours working out in the gym, shadow-boxing, skipping rope, punching bags. I had watched more than my share of pro fights, but I was not ready for what goes on up in that ring.

The butterflies started at the morning weigh-in. I wasn't afraid of getting hurt--bumps and bruises were an everyday occurrence. Nor was I afraid of losing. That's part of the game. But I was deathly afraid of getting booed. What if I was really lousy in there? The cat calls, the whistles, the boos! Drop out of school, that's what I'd do, or maybe stow away on a freighter!

Inside the dressing room, fight night. Collodion, spirits of ammonia, Absorbine Jr., adhesive tape, and nervous sweat.

Muffled roars, the barks of vendors, stomping feet, clanging bells and then, "Let's go, Napoleon, you're on!"

The club robe was draped over my shoulders as I walked down the aisle to the cheers of friends and well wishers. My opponent was already in the ring and now looked like a cross between Joe Louis and a sumo wrestler. 'I won't make myself anybody's laughing stock!' The bell sounded and out I came, swinging like a wild man. The first two minute round seemed like an eternity. I must have thrown 120 punches. I could barely walk back to my corner. If he hit me, I didn't feel it. If there were instructions from my seconds, I didn't hear them. I was too busy listening for boos. Things you worry most about never seem to happen. The fight was a real pier six brawl. After the fight money showered into the ring.

On our way home that night my dad told me he was very proud of my first victory. But even if I had lost the first, he said, he would still have been just as proud. I can still hear his words: "Anybody that steps into the ring or anywhere else and does the very best he knows how, he's a champ."

My father was quite a guy.

Chapter 10

If you ever have an itch to sail through the South Seas, the place to start would be the Ala Wai Yacht Harbor, just Ewa (west) of Waikiki. Beautiful boats from all over the world put in here. For some, it is a destination in itself. For others, a much needed rest stop before continuing their searches for that special paradise just beyond the horizon. Almost all use it to replenish supplies, make repairs, and replace crewmen grown weary of the arduous weeks and months at sea.

My father was an experienced seaman. From a 15-year-old stowaway on a tramp steamer to San Francisco, through a hitch in the U.S. Navy, ending up as a person on an inter-island steamship line, his pulse was tuned to the movements of every vessel in the harbor.

1946 had not been a good year, economically, in Hawaii. A long dock strike had hung up shipping and forced a business slowdown. A quick solution to the labor/management negotiations was not in sight. Complaints of shortages filled the pages of the newspapers, and radio newscasts echoed with the voices of doom. My father, however, looked on all this as a time of opportunity. He had his eye on a 100' cargo vessel that was in dire need of repair. It set in motion dreams of refurbishment and purchase, the beginnings of a shipping line.

He took a leave of absence from the life guards and chartered a 60' yacht. His plan was to go down to Tahiti and establish trade relations with the natives. More and more tourists were coming to our islands and grabbing up South Pacific artifacts and crafts, and the market for a venture of this kind could only grow. He had family on the Island of Tuamotu and was no stranger to the people and their ways.

We celebrated our good fortune with a big luau which finally ended down on the dock with flowered leis and music. We sang our alohas as he motored out of the harbor, set sail, and disappeared into the sunset.

A 60' boat is but a flyspeck on the open sea. Unpleasantries of any kind can take on nightmarish qualities and turn the loveliest of crafts into holes of hell. Once out of sight of land, the skipper became a tyrant, lashing out unmercifully at his crew and fighting with my father all the way down to the Tuamotus. Before he stepped on shore, however, my father had reduced the captain down to size and saw to it that the man would live up to his return contract or suffer the consequences the moment he set foot on the docks of Honolulu.

About three months later we met my father at the airport. He told us tales about lands of our beginnings and of the boatload of surprises he had in store for us. I remember getting up early each morning and racing for the docks and scanning the horizons for any sign of an incoming sail, though I knew the date of arrival was April 8. I was at home when the phone call came from the harbor. It was my father, the yacht had just tied up, so we piled into the big car and sped off down the hill.

Father was standing on the dock arranging bags and baggage and surrounded by the wildest looking group of Tahitians imaginable. As we approached, it became clear they were looking to him for some sort of guidance. My mother, walking next to me, squeezed my arm. Father looked up and saw us, motioned his colorful entourage to follow him and proudly began the introductions.

There was papa Ruau, an ancient firewalker, and his son-in-law Fati, so-called because of his tremendous girth. He weighed close to 300 pounds. Taiei, Huri and Turi were male dancers; they stepped forward, greeting us with overwhelming exuberance; Celestine and Fani, two very pretty girls, smiled shyly, eyes alive and heads slightly bowed.

Because the Tahitians could not speak English and we, of course, could not speak Tahitian, the conversation never got started. We just kept nodding at one another, picking up bags, loading them into and on top of the car. They never stopped singing all the way back to Punchbowl.

I remember my father telling my mother that a Tahitian firewalker was like money in the bank. People had never seen anything like this and his entire investment could be recouped in just three or four performances. Mother wasn't one to get upset easily but she was *hu hu*. All our money had gone for tickets and food to transport this troupe back to Hawaii, and the plot began to thicken. The firewalker refused to walk on the coals after sundown, something about religious taboos, and the power of fire, a fact that my father had unfortunately overlooked. At night of course was effect of the red glow would be spectacular, but in the daylight, not too good.

There was something very strange about this old man. He had an aura of mysticism about him and though he must have been at least 75, he possessed all the mannerisms and characteristics of a much younger man. I felt as though he knew what I was thinking. He kept 'looking out of the house, up towards Mt. Tantalus. He tapped his chest and pointed a finger at me and then motioned toward the lofty, green, cloud-shrouded peaks, and I knew he was telling me of his desire to go up into the mountains.

The city of Honolulu lay at our feet. I knew the trails well and we had arrived at a spot that afforded the most spectacular view in the islands. But he had not come up here as a sightseer. He was looking for something. Suddenly he bent down in a posture of attack. He shouted some Tahitian phrases and charged the ti leaf like a cat. He wrestled with it, tore the stalk from its trunk, holding it close to him as if in an embrace lovingly, and wrapped it in a towel. With closed eyes he swayed back and forth, chanting his words and phrases. He motioned to me that it was time to go now, and I led him back out of the forest and home.

The ti leaf branch he picked looked like a wishbone. Each branch is topped with green leaves and represents a woman. According to legend, these women were the goddesses of fire and protected him by casting a sp~ll on the coals and putting them to sleep. Like ghostly apparitions, they take on lifelike qualities. He really sees them and talks to them as he walks across the fire.

We leased the amphitheater up in Manoa. It's a good place to put on a show and it is surrounded by lush vegetation.

Advanced ticket sales went fairly well and by the time the entertainment was ready to start, we had a pretty good crowd.

The show opened with a Tahitian hevana. The musicians set up outside a circle of dancers seated boy-girl, boy-girl. Drums began to sound. Guitars and ukuleles picked up the rhythm then broke into the melody. A male dancer got up, jumped into the circle and began to dance. He moved towards one of the girls, took her hand and they danced wildly together. He sat down and she picked up a new partner. This was repeated around the circle.

The sun had another hour in the sky and the coals in the fire pit were red hot. Dad was still apprehensive over the fact that this gala event had to be held in the daylight. He kept assuring everyone that the fiery path would resemble a lava flow from a volcano, if only the damn sun would go down.

My premonition about the old man's ability to capture an audience, no matter what the hour, proved valid. He made his way through the crowd wearing a *pareau* and a necklace of sharks' teeth. His long, snowy-white hair billowed in the late afternoon breeze. The musicians took their cue and began a haunting drum chant. The fire walker picked up a coconut shell filled with some sort of alcoholic beverage and hurled it on the coals. The flames jumped four feet in the air and the audience howled with delight and anticipation; like Christ walking on the water, the fire walker effortlessly stepped across this burning mass of red hot coals.

"You should see it in the dark!" my father kept expounding over the applause.

The old man turned and retraced his steps. I felt a weird sensation come over me. The old man's eyes were upon me. He made his way to where I was sitting, extended his hand, and it was as if some invisible force brought me to my feet. I fell in behind him and we headed toward the coals.

By now, my father was coming unglued. This was going too far. He started to rise up in protest but two large Samoans, full of roast pig and Primo beer, placed their ham-like hands on his shoulders and pressed him back to earth.

All this time I was telling myself, 'If he gets burned, I get burned. If he can do it, I can do it. There's got to be some gimmick nobody takes chances like this!'

Before I knew it we had safely and painlessly negotiated the coals. But he did not stop here. Some twenty-odd people became his followers. Hawaiians, Haoles, tourists -- it made no difference. No one got burned.

My father got up and accepted the ovation from the crowd. "Please, everyone," he said, "stay away from the pit and give us a chance to smother the coals. Now we have more for you!"

The Tahitian dancers jumped up, the music rose to a torrid tempo. Then somewhere off to the side, raucous laughter and slurred words came from the crowd. A woman weaved her way toward the fire pit.

"The old man's nothing but a faker. Look at me, everybody! Go to sleep, you god-damned fire!"

Before anyone could reach her, she took a step and left the sole of her foot on a rock. She screamed and collapsed in pain, searing the flesh off her leg. One of the male dancers had a small mayonnaise jar chock-full of pearls. A few days after the show he and his pal picked up their belongings and disappeared. The old fire walker hung around the boat docks and found himself a ride on an old Tahiti ketch bound for the Tuarnotus and home.

The musicians found a job playing in a downtown bar, and that left us with the two dancers.

• • •

I was seventeen going on horny, and secretly hoped that these two would remain on with us forever. Real beauties they were, and sexy as only young Tahitian women can be. We swam and went to the park. They taught me to dance and sing Tahitian songs. Even my mother and sisters began to enjoy their company. They were a big help around the house and introduced us to some tasty cooking, Tahitian style.

We began to teach each other simple words and phrases. I learned to say 'screw' in Tahitian: *pic pic*. The girls thought this was hysterical. We would be sitting around, and one would tap her index finger on the table and say, "*pic pic*." We would laugh at our secret joke.

One night I took the girls to a burlesque show down on Hotel Street. I thought they would get a big kick out of watching the strippers perform. When an item of clothing was tossed off into the wings, they would clap their hands and stomp their feet. When the bumps and grinds reached a climactic stage, one of the girls reached over and grabbed me by the *ule*. With a mischievous smile she said, "You like *pic pic*?"

This was too much for me. I came unglued. I grabbed her hand away, at once confused, embarrassed and delighted. No sooner had I regained my composure than the other one grabbed me. By now I was convinced that everyone in the audience was looking at us. The lights came up and the show was over. Just in time.

That night, I was fitfully tossing and turning in my bed. No matter how hard I tried, sleep would not come. I kept thinking of what had happened to me that night in the theater. One more stripper, a little more time, and it would have been all over.

The curtains separating the living room from the lanai parted. The biggest of the two girls, Fani, was standing there in her nightgown. She came right to the bed, bent over, and kissed my cheek. I was petrified. She began working her tongue in my ear. "You like pic pic?"

She stood up and took off her nightgown. I couldn't believe it! This woman stood about 5'10"—broad hips, slim waist and boobs as big as my head. Christ! Her nipples were as big as my thumb. She rolled back the covers and began to kiss my chest, sucking on my nipples and running her tongue all the way down to my *kiko* and beyond. *Is she going to suck my ule?* The anticipation was insane. As she grabbed my *ule*, I could feel my sperm oozing out and dripping over her hand. She quickly put her mouth over my *ule*.

At seventeen, you can't take too much of this kind of treatment. She seemed to sense this and very quickly and easily jumped on top of me. Two or three skillful motions of her hips and I had an orgasm.

As she lay on top of me, I was still wallowing in ecstasy. I could feel her big boobs on my chest, my wet *ule* still deeply implanted inside her. She started to move again and we made love like a man and a woman.

In the morning the two girls were laughing and giggling in the kitchen. When I sheepishly appeared for breakfast, they smiled and the little one said, "You like *pic pic?*"

Chapter 11

A gentle trade wind blows me out to sea. The sun is warm on my back. I feel the cool water beneath me as my surfboard glides over tiny shorebound waves and ripples. My arms reach deeper into the blue-green water. Each stroke casts off a spray that rains against my face. The salty residue builds up on my lips, a tasty reminder of pleasures past. I push through a ragged line of white foam, the dying remains of a great wave that has thundered its last heroic gasp over a submerged coral reef. The scent of the sea intensifies my feeling of oneness with the ocean.

I begin to get beyond the bathers' playground. The paddling alone occupies me. Each incoming swell creates its own high. I pass the break at Queens, up, over and through the bigger frothing waves at Public Baths. A surfer, chased by a mountain of cascading water, screams across a huge vertical green wall at Castles. Exhilaration sets in, fed by intermittent shots of adrenalin. Past and future become now. I am suspended. I am free.

The morning's waves were still filtering down into my

memory as I walked across the park. A bunch of guys were throwing the football around. A long pass went astray and bounced toward me. I put my surfboard down and picked up the ball. I rocked back and put my foot into it. A lofty, high spiral that nosed over and carried for a good 55 yards. Satisfied, I walked on.

"Hey, wait a minute!"

I turned around. There was a kid running toward me as fast as he could go. "You talking to me?" I asked.

"The priest over there, *wid da kine* white collar, he like talk to you."

"I don't know any priest. What's he want with me?"

"I dunno. He just say he like talk to you, Nappy."

"Okay, okay," I replied. So I half walked, half ran, thinking, *Who the hell is this guy and what do I want with a priest, anyway?*

He was sitting on the fender of a car when I approached. "You wanted to see me?"

"Yes, I did. What's your name?"

"Napoleon. Hooulu Napoleon."

"Ho-who?"

"Hooulu. H-O-O-U-L-U."

"Do you have an English name?" he asked.

"You mean a *haole* name?"

"Yes."

"Yeah. Barry."

"Do you mind if I call you by your *haole* name?"

"No. Go ahead."

It sounded funny when he called me Barry. Too much like Mary. It was the first time that anybody outside of my immediate family had ever called me that. Local kids in school used to call me Oulu. (Even they had trouble with Hooulu.)

"Barry," I said. "That sounds okay by me."

"All right, then, Barry. I'll tell you what. If you can get hold of your birth certificate and bring it back to me, I'll give you $25."

"Are you kiddin' me?" I asked.

"Barry," he smiled, looking down at his black tunic, "You've got my word on that."

I ran all the way home and up the steps leading to my house at full speed. Bursting through the front door, I yelled, "Hey, mom! Where's my birth certificate?"

"What's all the excitement about?" my sister asked.

"I want my birth certificate. There's a priest down there at the park who's going to give me twenty-five bucks if I can prove I'm 16. Do you know where it is?"

"Yeah. Mother keeps it in the bureau."

I found the folded piece of paper buried underneath a pile of family records. I flew out the door and raced down the steps and never stopped until I got to the park. *Terrific*, I said to myself. *The guy's still there!*

"Here you are, bruddah! Here's my birth certificate! Now, where's my twenty-five bucks?"

"Barry, my name is Father Bray, and I'm the football coach at Iolani."

A wave of fear came over me. I was stunned. I had called the great Father Bray "bruddah". He was like a legend in Hawaii. He reached into his wallet and took out $25. "This is to let you know I'm a man of my word."

It was through Father Bray that I got a scholarship to Iolani. If it hadn't been for his guidance, I would probably have ended up on the streets.

At that time, high school football took on all the color and rivalry of big time college competition. Many times low scores registered on entrance exams were doctored if a boy possessed the physical ability to make high scores on the gridiron. The "High Mucky Mucks" didn't like to lose, and they didn't like their sons or daughters to lose.

In my first year at Iolani, I participated in everything: football. basketball. track, and swimming. School took on a whole new dimension. During the course of my senior year, offers of athletic scholarships began pouring in from the mainland. Because my family was Mormon, I decided on the University of Utah, with a freshman year of preparation at Weber College in Ogden.

Chapter 12

On the way down to the Matson docks, my mother was at it again. "Football playing is fine, but it's just a means to getting an education. That's what you're going to school for. An education. When you get home, the *haoles* will respect you. Remember to eat properly. And don't be getting any girls in trouble. Obey the rules. We know you will make us proud of you."

I answered with yeses, nos, and don't worrys and tried to act cool. I had watched the Lurline pull away from the dock countless times before, but usually from the water looking up. It was a great source of "walkin' around money." Yesterday, as kids, we would jump off the docks, swim alongside the great ship, and dive for coins or anything else the departing tourists would throw overboard. My mouth would get so loaded with loose change that my cheeks resembled those of a chipmunk gathering nuts. A sudden blast of steam served notice that the propellers were turning. We backstroked out of the mist and away from the churning water.

Now I was on the upper deck, looking down. The band began to play *Aloha Oe*. Streamers flew through the air. I spotted mother and father; she was wiping her eyes. I was already homesick.

Chapter 13

Dense fog rolled in from the Pacific. The visibility in downtown San Francisco was reduced to near zero. Fog horns moaned somewhere out on the bay. It was an eerie night. A rumble came up out of the ground, bells clanged, and a cable car slid cautiously down the hill. Four burly Hawaiian football players walked the streets of the city, freezing to death in damp aloha shirts and light cotton pants. It was mid-July in another world.

Chinese letters and anglicized names like "Canton Gardens", "The Ming Tree", "Hong Kong Fat", and "Kowloon" displayed in glowing neon were reduced to mist-shrouded halos. We found a haven from the cold in a small Chinese restaurant, drank hot tea, and consumed bowls and bowls of rice. The plane for Salt Lake would leave in the morning.

On board the flight, Charlie Kalani and Eli Kelahanui sat on one side of the aisle, Henry Gramburgh and I on the other. The stewardess attempted to read Eli's name off the ticket he handed her. We laughed. She got to Gramburgh and looked at him quizzically. Henry was 6' 4", weighed 245 pounds, and was half German, half Hawaiian. He told her he was Jewish.

• • •

Salt Lake City felt like a blast furnace. On the way to Ogden, some 35 miles to the north, the coach told us about what he called pre-season conditioning jobs. We would be digging irrigation ditches on a peach farm. The heat went on like that for the rest of the summer.

• • •

All the Hawaiian guys lived in a big dormitory. After the first few football games, we became known on campus as "The Dormitory Gang." The altitude was no longer a factor. Neither was the bone-dry air charged with static electricity. But with each passing day, the homesickness grew more acute. Our island ways never left us.

In celebration of the highly successful football season, a huge variety show was held in the school auditorium. The last entry on the program read:

A NIGHT IN HAWAI'I
with
THE DORMITORY GANG

Featuring:

Eli Kealanui
Charlie Kalani
Sonny Brae
Barry Napoleon
Bugala & Friend

The "friend" was a little Mexican gal we found. Eli taught her to do the hula. Our parents sent us leis wrapped in plastic bags and a few yards of tapa cloth. We were ready to go.

We took the stage with our guitars and ukuleles. When the crowd saw these big Hawaiian guys dancing and singing their way through *I Want To Go Back To My Little Grass Shack in Kealakekua, Hawaii*, they literally tore the place apart.

• • •

It turned cold in late November, the days grew short, and it started to snow. I had a hundred dollar bill that I guarded with my life. It was my mad money. I had to spend it on winter clothes so I could go outside.

One night, Henry and I bundled up and went down to 24th Street—the skid row section of town. There was a little Japanese restaurant sandwiched in amongst the cheap hotels, pool halls, and sleepy nighteries. The menu was hand-printed on a thin sheet of rice paper clipped between two stapled cardboard covers. "Kaimuki East," Henry said. "Home cookin'."

As we waited for our food, an argument started and three shadows began to tussle outside the steam-coated window. One was getting the shit kicked out of him. The restaurant owner stood behind the counter guarding the cash register and shouting in Japanese. Henry and I got up and went outside.

"Crook bastard! Gonna chase you back where you come from!" *Whack!* The little man went flying out into the street.

Henry and I had been cooped up in the dormitory too long. We exploded and tore into the first guy high-low. He cracked the ice on the sidewalk. The other one took off running and didn't get fifty feet. Two hundred forty-five pounds of Henry

Gramburgh smeared him like a cube of butter. I went over to the little guy and helped him to his feet. He was an Oriental and really shaken up.

"You alright, pal?"

"Yeah, I think so. Thanks, *brah*."

Now, the word "*brah*" is not something you'd expect to hear in a place like Ogden, Utah. "Man, that's Island talk, *brah*! Where you from?" I asked.

"Kalihi. But I been up here for 15 years."

Henry came walking back toward us, grinning from ear to ear. "That was kinda fun! You got any more where those come from?"

"I hope not! Let me buy you guys a dinner, huh?"

• • •

Back inside the restaurant, we sat down again and talked. His name was Castle, and he was one of the biggest gamblers in the state of Utah. He owned two illegal houses in Ogden, one in Salt Lake, and spent his spare time running back and forth to Las Vegas and Reno.

"I've watched you guys play football. You cost me a bundle the first game. I took the other team and gave 8 points. But I figure you repaid me in spades tonight." He paused for a moment. "You know, I could use a couple of guys like you. How'd you like to go to work for me?"

Castle was into everything and needed protection. From that point on, I would accompany him to Salt Lake when he had a big poker game. He carried twenty or sometimes thirty thousand on him. Henry and I became his watchdogs. The police in Ogden were always trying to bust him. When we saw them coming, lights went out, doors closed off the back room, and gamblers were herded into the cellar. It worked like the revolving sets on a theater stage. Eventually, word leaked out connecting Weber football players with gamblers and the curtain came down. But as it was, we had a lot of money to spend on Christmas presents that year.

Chapter 14

Winter turned to spring and people began popping out of doors like flowers out of the ground. I got a weekend job up in Ogden Canyon as a lifeguard and bartender. Lamadrid, a Filipino kid from Hawaii, was a halfback on the football team and was working as a bus boy. One morning, he came to work sporting a shiner.

"Was it worth it?" I asked him.

"Easiest twenty-five bucks I ever made."

"Twenty-five bucks? What're you talkin' about?"

I met him down by the railroad yard the following Friday. We hopped a freight train and rode all day to Boise. It was fight night. Weigh-ins for standby fighters were held at 5 o'clock. A doctor put a stethoscope to your chest, told you to jump up and down on one leg, and if your heart didn't stop, you passed. They paid five dollars a round, twenty-five if you went the distance, four rounds. They even had extra trunks and shoes. I gave them a phony name, told 'em I was from Salt Lake, and waited.

My friend was already on the program and he assured me

that he'd see to it that it was a short night. He'd finish the guy in one, he said, and he remained true to his word. The fight lasted 40 seconds into the first round and they carried the opponent into the dressing room. A panicked promoter told me to strip down. I was on in five minutes.

My opponent was a big *popolo* guy. He already had his gear on and looked like he'd had 500 fights too many. His eyes never left me as he warmed up in the corner, shadow boxing to the rhythm of a sing-song jingle:

> *Juba dis*
> *'n' juba dat*
> *Juba killed a yellow cat*
> *'n' bought hisself a Sunday hat*

We got our instructions up in the ring and he glared into my face. When we touched gloves, he said, "Ain't no niggers in heaven." I went four rounds with him, but it was the hardest twenty-five bucks I ever made.

We rode another freight back to Ogden that same night. I remember passing a store window walking home from the depot. My face was covered with soot. I was black-faced like Al Jolson.

Chapter 15

After 22 hours on a greyhound bus, anything looks good—even the murky waters of the oil-coated, junk-filled East Bay. School was out and the Golden Gate was just ahead. Henry and I were going home for the summer.

The Lurline, majestically awaiting a full complement of passengers, looked like a dream come true. The dock was jammed with eager, friendly faces. This was going to be some trip.

An ensemble of Island entertainers, singers, dancers and musicians, played the old familiar standards as the tug boats pulled the ship away from shore.

"Henry, you dumb shit! Nobody dresses for dinner the first night out!"

He looked at me like I was crazy. "I'm not dressin' up. Whatssa matta you?"

He was putting on his first clean clothes since the agonizing bus ride—clean pants and an aloha shirt, wrinkled up like prunes. We had a tiny compartment down on E deck. It was so far below the waterline, the pressure hurt your ears. I opened my suitcase and the heat from the hot bus ride radiated off my crumpled clothes. It was Henry's turn to laugh.

"Hey, Nap. We're gonna give those high mucky mucks up on A deck a real lesson in sartorial splendor tonight, huh?"

"Sartorial splendor! Say, your mama's gonna be proud of you!"

"What you think? I spent a whole year at college and didn't learn nothin?"

The Lurline was lit up like a floating roman candle. Kids from all over the U.S. are dancing the same steps, singing the same songs, and thinking the same thoughts. This is the most romantic place in the whole world.

Lovely hula hands, graceful as the birds in motion…

Two girls in fresh ti leaf skirts dance the hula. Joe Kealoha and his Islanders, with professional smiles and practiced enthusiasm, ease right into *Keep Your Eyes on the Hands*. The girls use this as an opportunity to demonstrate their ability to throw their hips around.

"Bet those guys have sung that song ten-thousand times." It's Henry again. "When's somebody gonna write somethin' different?"

The girls sink to the floor and graciously accept the hearty applause. The tourists love it. House lights dim and drums begin to pound. Henry knows what's coming and lets out a "*Ho'o Pa'a!*" Two spotlights pick up the shimmying girls, and they move their hips like trip hammers. They pass by ringside tables picking out unlikely male partners. The chosen guys walk reluctantly out on the floor, put their hands behind their heads and lasciviously go into awkward bumps and grinds.

One of the girls spots Henry. They'd grown up together in Kailua. He is a great dancer. She walks him up out of the audience, he throws off his shirt, and away they go. Her partner, not to be outdone, grabs me. The crowd goes wild.

The floor show is over and the after-dinner dancers take over. Henry and I, wringing wet, head for the bar.

All the excitement, the booze, the dancing, the milling crowds, closed in on me and I made my way up to the top deck for some fresh air.

As I walked along the deck, breathing deeply and looking up at the cloud formations so white against the evening sky, I noticed a lady standing all alone. She was wearing a beautiful white gown, her hair was done up tightly in a bun, and a diamond necklace twinkled like stars around her neck. I stopped a few feet from her and leaned up against the rail, noting in the process a slim silver wedding band guarded by an enormous sapphire. She was the most elegant-looking woman I had ever seen in my life.

The moon shone down, illuminating the ship's wake like a glowing fire. It produced the same hypnotic effect.

"Beautiful night, isn't it?" I said, unable to pull my eyes away from the churning phosphoresce.

"Gorgeous. Simply gorgeous," she answered.

We turned and looked over at one another in perfect synchronization. She had a pretty face, though I could tell some of the warmth of youth had grown cold with advancing years. I guessed her to be somewhere around 45.

"Aren't you the young man I saw dancing the hula after dinner?"

"Yeah. That was me."

Young man. I hated that. When you're young, it's a put down. It places the person that says it in the role of an authoritative figure. But, from the looks of her, I guess that's what she was.

"Are you a part of the show?"

"No. Just a passenger like yourself."

"Wouldn't you rather be down there enjoying all the fun?" she asked.

"Too much of a good thing all at once. I needed a breather." Privately, I wondered if maybe she was politely trying to tell me something, like get lost. "Don't worry. I'm game. I'm going back for more."

"Good. And I'm not worried. The fact of the matter is I envy the hell out of you."

"Then what are you doin' up here all alone?"

"I'm afraid I've reached the age of inactive participation. To have stayed any longer would have placed me in the position of a voyeur."

"People are just dancing. Do you like to dance?"

"I love to dance, but it's not often I get the opportunity."

"You got it. C'mon, I'll take you dancing."

"Darling, I'd be much too self-conscious to enjoy myself. But you are a dear for asking."

"You afraid of what people might think?"

"Yes, you might say that. And other things."

"I don't know about the other things, but nobody's up here. The music's the same, only softer. Would you like to dance?"

Now you've done it, I said to myself. *This chick's gonna put you in your place, walk off, and spend the rest of the night tossing and turning in her bunk.* But instead, she looked all around, saw we were very much alone, and said, "Yes. Yes. I think I would like that very much."

I took her in my arms. The vocalist just below us was singing the lyrics of a Doris Day tune:

> *Gonna take a sentimental journey*
> *Gonna set my heart at ease*
> *Gonna take a sentimental journey*
> *And renew old memories*

"Now, tell me," I said, "who you are, where you're comin' from, and what you're gonna do when you get there."

"Blunt, but to the point. I like that. All right. I'm from San Francisco. I'm the wife of a very successful lawyer. My mother is traveling with me, and also my sister. And I have a daughter who is getting married a week from Saturday on the Island of Kauai. How's that for a quick resume?"

"Quick. And your husband. I take it he's not with you."

"You *are* inquisitive, aren't you?"

"Just trying to keep it honest."

"No, he's not with me. He's much too busy to waste five days on a boat. He's flying in later on in the week."

"Do you miss him?"

"I've missed him for 15 years."

The music continued…

> *Get you and keep you in my arms ever more*
> *Leave all your worries waitin' on some faraway shore*

She put her head on my shoulder and I felt her lower body press more firmly against me. I began to grow hard and she pushed harder. "Mmmmm," she said. "You really know how to dance."

Our feet stopped shuffling and we swayed in time to the music. When it stopped, I held both her hands in mine and slowly stepped backward. I was almost bursting out of my pants. She looked down at me. Her hand slipped out of mine and she eased them very lightly back and forth between my hips and up and down from my belt to well beneath my crotch. I unzipped my fly and there it was.

"Oh, god!" she sighed. "I don't even know your name! What's happening to me?" She squeezed me with love-starved delight. She raised up on her toes. We kissed and clung to each other. She trembled and whispered, "Make love to me. Oh, please make love to me."

I ripped a pad from a lounge chair and led her up to the paddle tennis court, opened the gate, and right there in front of the moon and the stars and the King of the Universe, we lay down. It was a moment in time that I can never forget.

Chapter 16

Every morning, Donny Lord and I jogged around the ship for exercise. We were old track competitors in high school and, during the summers at Waikiki, we used to have races on the beach. I was a sprinter and he was a middle distance man. He always ended up chasing me.

Donny liked to talk a lot. He could gab his way right out of a piece of ass. I knew he hadn't been getting any action, and the day before the boat was due to arrive in Honolulu, he asked me about the Colonel's wife. We called her "The Colonel's Wife," even though she was still a single lady. Her fiancee, a Colonel in the Army, had been transferred from Ft. Hood, Texas to Schofield. They were going to be married just as soon as she got to Honolulu. I learned all this the second night out. We met in the bar, ended up in her stateroom, and I'd been doing a secret number with her on that voyage ever since.

Outside her cabin doors, we appeared as two casual shipboard friends, but Donny knew me and was suspicious.

"Have you ever screwed her?" he questioned.

"What do you think?" I said, breaking into a mischievous smile.

He studied me a moment. "Ha! You're shittin' me!" he said.

"Donny, would I shit you?"

That night after dinner, a gang of us gathered up on the top deck for a ukulele session. We sang our favorite island songs and made promises to each other that this would not be the end of the friendships we had formed. The orchestra began to play on the deck below and, one by one, our little group began to disband until just three of us remained: Donny Lord, the Colonel's Wife, and myself. Donny began talking like a madman in a vain effort to score some last minute points. *There he goes again*, I thought to myself, *talking himself right out of a piece of ass.*

"Let's go downstairs and dance," the Colonel's Wife suggested, putting a temporary stopper on Donny's endless dialogues.

The three of us stood together at the edge of the dance floor. She tugged on my arm, and we moved out into the crowd. Halfway through the medley, I felt a tap on my shoulder.

"Can I cut in?" It was Donny.

They must have danced for a good ten minutes. The band took five and they walked off the floor towards me. Donny excused himself to go to the men's room, assuring us he would be right back.

"Your friend certainly is persistent," she said to me. "He talked my little ol' ear off. Let's go have a drink. I need one after that!"

On our way to the bar, an announcement was made that the volcano on the Big Island of Hawaii had erupted. The Captain was changing course, and we would be passing the Island at

10:00 pm. From all reports, the view would be spectacular.

• • •

It felt like an oven outside. Billows of smoke poured into the atmosphere. Fiery red lava exploded out of the mountain. Molten rivers flowed into the sea. Volcanic cinders rained down from above like the residue from a tremendous skyrocket. The shoreline was shrouded in hissing steam. We passed through the smoke-laden air currents and into light winds scented with flowers. It was the unmistakable aroma of our Islands—a fragrance at once so meaningful to me that it brought tears to my eyes. I took hold of the bride-to-be's hand.

"Close your eyes and take a deep breath. Can't you just see all those beautiful flowers?"

"Sort of. I was wondering what that smell was," she said.

I took her back to her room and we made love. I told her not to worry; if she fell asleep, I would let myself out.

It was after 2:00 a.m. when I stepped out of the cabin and into the gangway. I blinked my eyes to get accustomed to the light. She had an inside stateroom, and those things were absolutely pitch black. But then, who did I see corning at me, but my old pal, Donny—his last night out and obviously unsuccessful again.

"Hey, Donny," I whispered. "Come here."

He walked up and stood right next to me, whispering, "Where did you guys go? I've been looking all over for you!"

"Never mind that now. The Colonel's Wife is right inside, waiting for you."

"Are you shitting me?" he said.

"Donny, would I shit you?" I put my hand on his shoulder,

looked up one end of the hall and down the other, and added, "But Donny, one thing: don't say a word."

He gave me a funny look, then opened the door just wide enough to slip through, and quietly closed it behind him. He got out of his clothes and slipped into bed beside her. Sure enough, she was waiting for him, asleep but nude.

His attempts at a penetration awakened her. "Oh, Nappy... you feel so good."

Donny didn't say a word, he just kept on going. When he got up to leave, she turned on the light. There was Donny with his pants down. She was stunned. "You sonovabitch! Get out of here!"

• • •

The next morning, we were off Diamond Head. Tug boats steamed out to meet us. So many people were lined up on the decks, the big ship actually appeared to be listing. Canoes full of beach boys paddled by, flowered leis floated on the water. One crazy kid, returning from school, dove off the top deck and swam, fully clothed, to meet his buddies. They don't make welcomes like that any more.

When the boat docked, Donny and I were standing together, the last night's escapade rehashed and laughed at. Our mutual girlfriend made her way toward us. "You two are, without a doubt, the most despicable, unprincipled, no-good bastards I've ever met in my entire life—and I'm madly in love with you both!"

The Spirit of Aloha was everywhere. She took each of us by an arm and we walked down the gangplank to meet the Colonel.

Chapter 17

"Danthers! Danthers! Where are my danthers?"

The choreographer was a flaming *mahu*. We'd been spending two weeks up at Kamehameha School learning to do the Hawaiian hula under the watchful eye of Iolani Nuawahine, the finest hula teacher in the Islands. More than 100 answered the casting call for "Hawaiian types to portray South Sea natives in the upcoming motion picture *Bird of Paradise*, starring Jeff Chandler, Debra Padgett, and Louis Jordan. Thirty of us were chosen. We spent the better part of the next week staging the big dance number and learning to mouth the words of chants, which were already pre-recorded on a soundtrack. With a few minor exceptions, the work resembled one big party.

We were flown to the Big Island on chartered planes. The film company had built an entire village at Kepoo. It was complete in every respect. There was even a common house. (Before the white man arrived and "civilized" us, the common house was used for marital test trials. A boy and a girl would try each other on for size and if they were suited for one another, they married. If it was a bad match, forget it.)

It took a full day to block out the dance sequence. A second day was used for a camera run-through. They had a camera on a crane and cameras moving in and out set on crab dollies—the "picture-taker that moves on wheels", as one beach boy called them.

"Eight o'clock tomorrow morning, kidths! Everyone!"

That's some job, I thought to myself. *Big title like Choreographer, and all he does is yell times and places through a bullhorn.*

The next morning, it rained and they rescheduled shooting for the following day.

The next morning was the big day. The director was dressed for a jungle safari. "This is going to be our master shot, people! We are going to film the dance in its entirety. Try to remember your places and, if you must pick your nose or scratch your ass, for God's sake, remember where you were in your routine at the time! We want your close-ups to match! Have fun, people, and break a leg!"

A man ran out in front of us with a blackboard topped by two pieces of wood that clap together.

"Sound ready! Roll speed!"

"Speed rolling!"

"Paradise 56, Take 1!"

"Music up and…action!"

All morning we danced and danced. We would just get going and the director would yell, "Cut!" We broke for lunch. "Jesus Christ, people! Let's get it right this time!"

The director went over to the cameraman. "We're wasting too fucking much time on this fucking thing! Let the fuckers do their fucking dance all the fucking way through. Any fucking mistakes we can pick up in the fucking close-ups!"

"Now, for Christ sake, people! Look like you're having a good time!"

"Roll speed!"

"Speed rolling."

"Paradise 56, Take 15!"

"Music up and...action!"

This time we really got into it. Half-way through the number the dolly started moving by. As it passed in front of one of the guys, he raised his two arms in the air and grabbed ahold of a branch that was hanging over his head. He hung there by one hand and scratched himself under the other arm, screeching like a monkey.

"Shit Almighty! Cut it! And get that asshole out of there!"

• • •

Later that summer, I acted in another movie called *Twilight of the Gods*. I played the part of a policeman. There was a fight scene, a tussle in the sand, and I had to get up and chase a guy along the beach. Once again, as in the other picture, we were made to do it over and over. When the movie was released, the lousy buggers had cut the whole thing out.

Chapter 18

The Jet Age hadn't been invented yet, and it took 14 hours to fly from Honolulu to the mainland. Pan American flew a big Stratocruiser with two levels and sleeping berths. Transocean had a nonscheduled flight that resembled an airborne cattle car. United went to San Francisco and L.A. It was usually loaded with businessmen carrying briefcases and wearing important faces. They offered first class, tourist class, continental cuisine, and exotic booze. But it was all the same: flaming propellers, fasten-your-seatbelt signs, and wrinkled pants. In those days, the boat was too much fun, and time didn't matter a damn.

The first time I saw her, she was leaning against the ship's rail, black hair flying in the late afternoon breeze, gazing out to sea. Oahu was still visible on the horizon, but rapidly losing its battle to stay afloat. A wayward gust of wind found its way beneath her white cotton skirt, lifting it high, exposing summer-tanned legs and brief silk panties. I felt like I had just been hit by a highly charged wave. *Jeezus! What a wahine!* She pushed the billowing skirt back down and caught me staring.

At home, on the beach, I would have moved right in with a smart remark. Here, I felt strangely ill at ease. My confidence was still back on Kalakaua Avenue. I smiled in an attempt at nonchalance and looked back in the direction of my Island. I suddenly felt all alone in the world. When I turned her way again, she was gone.

The boat was loaded with college kids going back to school. First night parties were going on everywhere. An open stateroom door was an open invitation. Chubby Mitchell and I made the rounds together. He was about 5'7" and must have weighed close to three hundred pounds. He was as black as the ace of spades, as jolly as Santa Claus, and every bit as generous. Such a proud Hawaiian he was. He carried his ukulele with him wherever he went and could play and sing Island songs like no one else.

It was getting late. Time and heavy-handed measures of alcohol compounded to take the edge off the earlier excitement. We were in a large outside stateroom and Chubby had the last of the hangers-on mesmerized with his rendition of *I'll Remember You*. I felt proud to be his pal.

"Hi, there, you peeping Tom. Mind if I squeeze in here next to you?" It was the girl with the blowing skirt and the tan legs. I moved to make a bigger space for her, but not too big.

"Thank you," she whispered. She smelled like she just stepped out of a scented bath.

The song ended. Chubby was in need of a nutrition break. He caught my eye, put the uke under his arm, made a circle with the thumb and index finger of his left hand, and stuck the middle finger of his right hand through it. He smiled, grabbed a handful of small rice cakes, and walked out the door. My head spun 360 degrees on my shoulders to see if anyone had caught his gesture. No one seemed to have noticed a thing—with the exception of bright eyes sitting next to me.

"Friend of yours?" she asked.

"Oh, that's just Chubby. Great kidder, that guy."

"That's too bad."

"What's too bad? That he's a friend of mine?"

"No, that you thought he was kidding. I've been lusting after your bod for years."

Christ! This was unreal!

"You know me?"

"Of course. You're Barry, and we have a couple of very close mutual friends. Girl friends."

"You live in Honolulu?"

"All my life. Born and raised."

"How come I never met you before this?" I studied her face. The smooth texture of her skin. I liked what I saw, and she knew it.

"You should have tried coming around the Outrigger some time."

That was a touchy subject, and she realized it the moment she said it. They don't take to Kanakas hanging around the Outrigger.

"Well, I blew that one, didn't I?" she said. She pulled her knees up and clasped her hands around them. Her thighs rubbed against mine.

"Ain't no big thing. The Outrigger's back there and we're here."

She put her hand on the back of my neck, her fingers

nestled in my hair, and I bent down and kissed her. Right there in the middle of the stateroom floor. Right there in front of all those *haoles*.

• • •

We stood on the upper deck and watched the dawn come up. Her name was Mary Ann and she was a direct descendent of one of the old missionary families. We talked of our upbringings and discovered mutual feelings of discontent festering within us. Co-conspirators destined to right the wrongs of an errant society. She was on her way to Pasadena City College to make up some credits before going on to USC.

"S.C. was my parents' preference. I hear it's a big WASP school. Hell, I should have gone to Berkeley. But no, I go right along with their wishes. Don't rock the boat, Mary Ann. Some rebel, huh?"

"Hey, don't come down so hard on yourself. Things change."

The conversation was getting pretty heavy and it was too beautiful outside to spoil. I headed her off in another direction. She was ready, for she picked right up on it.

"You know, my brother Alan's on board. He's going to Pasadena. Gonna play football for them."

"How neat! Will you introduce me?"

"I don't know. Think you could handle more than one Hawaiian at a time?"

"Might be fun to try." She came right back at me. No doubt about it, this was a special girl.

We ate all day and danced all night. There were games, there was laughter. Many drinks and more Chubby Mitchell songs. By the time we docked in LA, I was in love.

My brother Alan could talk as good a game as he played. A few days before leaving Honolulu, he fell off a horse and broke his arm. The head coach at Pasadena and his assistant had made the long trek across town to meet the boat in San Pedro. When they saw his cast, they almost fainted. Alan introduced me to the horrified pair and assured them it was only a minor break. The cast was due to come off in a couple of weeks, but should any unforeseen complications arise, he had brought me along to fill in for him. "With helmets on, you won't be able to tell us apart." The two crewcut coaches were speechless, and I went right along with the gag. A few days' delay in getting to Utah would not make a heck of a lot of difference and, besides, I could look Mary Ann up and continue where we left off.

It was a quiet ride all the way to Pasadena. We stopped for dinner, and coaches Blackman and Musick proceeded to tell us of the advantages of playing for a school like Pasadena.

Coaches are born salesmen. They felt they had a shot at the Little Rose Bowl and, both being alums of SC, their players had an inside track to the big time. They began to stoke themselves. "Notre Dame, the Coliseum, crowds of 105,000, national fame." It was every athlete's dream. We scrimmaged all morning and, afterwards, I was escorted to the administration office and enrolled with a better deal than I had at Utah.

A football season means ten Saturdays of pain interspersed with five less glorious days of more pain. Then, before you know it, it's December and all over. But for me, the real pain had just begun. The night after our last game, Mary Ann informed me that she was pregnant.

Abortion was out of the question in those days. A pal of

mine had been through it with his girlfriend. It meant Tijuana, a cheap hotel room, the dreaded knock on the door, and a doctor with questionable credentials and an eye for an illicit buck. It meant pain, fear of infection, and even the risk of death. Mary Ann wanted no part of that and neither did I.

The West Coast's answer to premarital problems of any kind—be they parental disapproval, backseat recklessness, or even midnight madness—could be found in Reno or Las Vegas. Southern Californians went to Las Vegas. A flashing arrow, set just off the main thoroughfare, pointed to an all-night chapel that was lit up like a gaudy Christmas tree. The marquee offered a best man, a recording of the ceremony, and a photographer at a slight extra charge. In fifteen minutes, it was all over. Being the holiday season, rooms were at a premium, so we spent our wedding night retracing tire tracks through the desert back to Pasadena.

December 31: Doomsday. Mary Ann called her parents to break the news. The connection was bad—electronically and emotionally—at both ends. Her mother was catching the next plane. And by the way, Happy New Year.

That night I got drunk. Oh boy, did I get drunk. I drank all night. The alarm went off at 7 a.m. Stanford was playing Illinois in the Rose Bowl. I was an usher and had to be at the stadium at nine o'clock. My new mother-in-law was arriving in L.A. at ten o'clock, and Mary Ann was fit to be tied because I wouldn't go with her to pick up her mother. I explained to her that this was probably the only chance I'd ever get to see a Rose Bowl game and I wasn't about to miss it.

Every time I took someone up and down those steps, I was stricken with the dry heaves. Shortly after the kickoff, I forced down a hotdog and a coke. I lost that on the way back to my station. I will remember that game as long as I live.

"Will Barry Napoleon please report to the Stadium Office!"

The second half had just begun. Mary Ann and her mother were waiting for me in front of the stadium. What a first impression I must have made: I was unshaven, hung-over, and had traces of puke down the front of my front shirt.

"God in heaven, Mary Ann! What have you done? He's black!"

"Not black, lady. Brown."

"And not married to my daughter, either!" she shot back. "We're seeking an annulment first thing in the morning. And you, you Kanaka! You can just go back and continue doing whatever it was you were supposed to be doing!"

"Mamma," Mary Ann cried, "There's something you don't understand! I'm pregnant!"

"Mary Ann, call me a cab!"

The smoke cleared and the sobs subsided. The room was growing dark and outside an unusually heavy flow of traffic was using our narrow street as an escape route from the tens of thousands of cars caught in the post game exodus. We sat side by side on the Woolworth Modern couch, staring at the wall. What came next was like a giant salvo going off in my ears. Each word thundered through my brain. "I'm not pregnant. I never was pregnant. I did it because I love you. I never thought it would end up this way. I wanted you so much. Can you understand that?"

"I'm tryin', sweetheart. I'm trying."

We made love on the floor, we made love on the bed. We went out for hamburgers, came home, and made love again. We made Mary Ann pregnant. The special delivery letter read: "We have made a reservation for you at the Moana Hotel. Advice is cheap. Enclosed, find check." It was signed by Mary Ann's father.

The atmosphere around the dinner table was icy cold. My mother-in-law and I exchanged only the most formal of generalities. Mary Ann's dad reminded me of a time-worn ice breaker relentlessly trying to break a path through an endless frozen sea. I could see Mary Ann was stretched between a chasm that would only grow wider and at some time must make a decision as to which side to hang on to. When her parents left on a world cruise, we moved into the big house on Diamond Head. As she grew larger with the child inside her, the comforts and amenities of her old familiar surroundings began to take on new meaning. Our future, a small one-room apartment in Waikiki, became more foreboding.

I bought her a large *muumuu* to cover her *opu*, and when her parents returned from their cruise, it took me ten trips up and down the stairs to unload all the packages they had brought for her. We moved back to Waikiki and our time together waiting for the baby's arrival became an endurance contest. It was noisy, it was hot, it was confining, and my attempts at finding meaningful employment were disappointing. A trip to Moiliili was a big night out for us.

• • •

Six weeks after the birth of my son, she walked out and never returned. I quit my job. I quit that lousy apartment. I hung out on the street looking for ways to turn a fast buck. I got a job working for a landscaping firm, doing exhausting manual labor. I would come home, pour a few pieces of booze, and drink myself to sleep. I felt like I had been set adrift in the doldrums. One day faded into the next. Listlessness and depression set in. Pent-up emotions screamed for release. I started arguing and fighting with my friends and continued to brood over the break-up of my marriage and the uncertain role, if any, I would ever be allowed to play in my child's future.

Big trouble was looming in front of me. I have always loved the beach in the early morning. It's clean and peaceful. The atmosphere cleanses my every pore and I experience a feeling of total well being. It is my best time. It is such a special place. If anyone was looking for me, they could always count on finding me there, having coffee with the guys, watching the waves, delaying thoughts of what I was going to do with the rest of the day, with the rest of my life.

"Hey, you! Napoleon! Get over here! Big as you are, I can still give you a lickin'!"

I whirled around. My dad was parked by the curb, leaning out of the window, showing his fist. He got out of the car. We moved toward each other and met center ring on the sidewalk of Kalakaua Avenue. We bobbed and weaved, throwing near misses at one another.

"You're lookin' sharp as ever," he said. "C'mon, take a ride with me. I got to go to the country."

I welcomed the opportunity to escape from myself for a few hours, though I suspected there would be more to this trip than his desire for company. My dad was usually a solitary man.

As we drove through the city of Honolulu, just now corning alive with the people who keep the wheels turning, it became more and more apparent that my father had something on his mind and was using this long drive to muster his thoughts together. The road skirted Pearl Harbor and the Naval shipyards. The rusting hulk of the U.S.S. Arizona recalled to mind the strange plight of my Japanese grandfather.

Many years ago, the rich plantation owners looked to Japan as a source of cheap labor to work their fields. Grandfather was a small boy but strong and sturdy enough to do a man's work. He was allowed to make the journey to Hawaii with his parents. Our growing season never ends, and the family stayed on. When he was a young man, his mother sent his photograph to relatives in Japan and, as was the custom in those days, the family selected a Japanese wife for him and put her on a boat bound for Honolulu. My grandfather, in the interim, had been waiting around a long time, communications were bad, so he took conjugal matters into his own hands and married an Island girl.

Never one to shun a contractual obligation, he married the young Nipponese girl as soon as she arrived, and promptly impregnated her. He apparently liked his new way of life, for he took on another wife, the last being my grandmother. They all lived in the same house at the same time and bore children like a tree bears fruit. Soon after the birth of her second child, the Japanese wife grew tired of his communal living arrangements and returned to her homeland. Whether or not he found her to be his true love will always be a mystery.

The air began to grow heavy with the sweet sugary scent of pineapples and burning sugar cane. Rush hour traffic on the Kam Highway all but disappeared and dad began to open up.

"I understand all of your hurt, but I cannot help you with it. Only time can cure this hurt you're feeling. You must always try to be a man, no matter what you feel inside. If you remember this, you're going to always come out on top."

The lush green canefields, like dad's lecture, were behind us now. Big waves were breaking off Barbers Point. The weather was becoming hotter and drier. We had reached the leeward side of the island. As we approached the small seaside community of Nanakuli, my father broke the silence that had enveloped us.

"My business out here is not that important. In fact, I think my days are mixed up. Been a long time since we've been together like this. Let's pick up a couple of boards at your uncle's house and go to Makaha. The waves look good today."

That day was a turning point of sorts in the relationship with my father. It got better. He treated me like a grown-up from then on. He felt my hurt, and I knew it. I never forgot his advice that day, and we had a different kind of understanding between us from then on.

Chapter 19

I got a job putting on luaus for the Niu Malu Hotel. It was a Friday job. I dressed the tables with flowers and leaves and cooked the pig. The whole thing paid $20 a week. I sold encyclopedias during the day and at night became a bouncer in a Waikiki night club. Then, like a geographic drunk, I reasoned that if I got away from this place—if I left Hawaii and all my problems behind—things would get better. Accompanied by my constant companions, hostility and frustration, I went down to the airline office and booked a flight to California.

My brother was living in Alameda and got me a job at the California Packing Company, loading and unloading boxes of canned goods. The pay was excellent and the long hard hours of physical labor began to reduce the size and scope of my problems back home. One day, a fight broke out in the warehouse. It turned into a wild, fist-swinging melee. I was in the middle and it took three big, powerful guys to restrain me. They didn't have to fire me. I quit.

I threw hot rivets making girders for bridges and buildings and thought of home. One morning, the Los Angeles Times ran an article on the fantastic uranium deposits being uncovered on the Colorado Plateau. The Atomic Energy Commission (A.E.C.) was offering a guaranteed market at a guaranteed price for a period of ten years, plus a discovery bonus of $10,000. It was a rainbow's end for the green-horned treasure seeker. I went about collecting maps and literature. I visited war surplus stores and rock shops and returned home with mimeographed price lists of geiger counters, probes, hammers, scintillometers, ore sacks, and standard uranium ore samples.

I went to my father and brother, told them of my plans, and reinforced them with the success stories pouring out of the Canyonlands. Blind enthusiasm smacked into the wall of reason and our discussions turned to arguments. If they thought this was sheer madness, so be it. I would go it alone. It was a chance and—who knows?—somewhere out there a bonanza possibly awaited someone willing to accept the risks.

The very next day, my brother Walter called. He said he had a two-week vacation coming up. He would go with me. My father would help defray expenses. They still thought I was crazy, but crazy schemes have been known to work out. Anyway, we could always sell the equipment, so what did we have to lose but—wait…they got snakes out there?

• • •

Six a.m., the California-Arizona border: the temperature gauge hanging on the wall of a Needles gas station read 95 degrees. Intense heat in the Arizona desert threatened to melt the rubber off the tires. The car boiled over; it was a pre-war DeSoto. Our brains began to fry.

Nightfall found us in Flagstaff at a cheap diner with

tasteless, greasy food. We bedded down in an empty boxcar on a siding just outside the railroad yard.

North through Navajo land. Tall cactus, red desert, mud hogans, with derelict automobiles upside down in the junk-cluttered yards. An old woman tended a few scraggly sheep. We stopped for cokes and gas at a small trading post out in the middle of nowhere. A few Indians—long pigtails, black hats, and cowboy shirts—leaned up against an old Plymouth. They looked at us with challenge in their eyes. Maybe they thought we were Comanches.

On and on past hot, dusty, isolated little towns separated by vast distances of emptiness and burning rock: Mexican Hat, Bluff, Blanding, Monticello, and finally, Moab, Utah. The town was swollen with would-be prospectors. House trailers, old cars, and war surplus jeeps were jammed into every available parking space and vacant lot. Hastily hand-painted signs proclaiming "Mining Information Inside" stood against dust-covered plate glass windows.

Hot and dirty, we walked into a crowded tavern and drank watery 3/2 beer. Information was free for the listening. We learned Mormons have few compunctions about separating a Gentile from his money. Firearms were damn good things to carry in the back country; mountain lions and snakes—both animal and human—were everywhere.

A jeep trail wound for fifty miles over tire-busting, axle-breaking, clutch-burning terrain. Helicopters from big mining companies occasionally soared overhead. My brother, already wearing of this adventure, suggested that maybe they were trying to tell us something. We left the car and walked 'til sundown.

This place was not for human beings. It suffocated. It sucked the juices out of you. I looked over at my brother, Walter, and what I saw pained me. His shirt was stained with perspiration. He'd removed a boot and poked at one of a cluster of sore, water-filled blisters. I took a drink of warm water from my canteen. It smacked of metal. I thought of the two of us body surfing at Makapuu on a perfect six-foot day; of reefs alive with fish; of waterfalls pouring into limpid pools ringed with cool, sweet mountain apples—ours for the taking.

We spent more than a week and a half living an almost animal-like existence. In all that time, we came upon just three people: a man, his wife, and small child who were living under a tarpaulin stretched between two cottonwood trees. There was a spring nearby, as big as a bathtub, and he had blasted a pit toilet in the ground with two charges of powder. The needle on my geiger counter never moved.

Hawaiians don't give up easily, no matter how they're hurting. Abandoned mine shafts bored into the sides of mountains looming up behind the old mining towns of Ouray, Silverton, Buena Vista, and Leadville told tales of tungsten from hangers-on still prowling the back country of the Sangre de Cristo Range and back up into the high country.

It was cold above 10,000 feet. Hearts pounded, and lungs worked overtime. Smoke rose from an old tin funnel protruding from the roof of a small, weatherbeaten cabin. A scraggly old codger appeared at the doorstep—a log cut flat and laid horizontally across rounded stumps. The shirt of his union suit appeared to grow out of his body, its pungent odor kept cutting into our conversation. He called us greenhorns, and laughed when we told him of our plans to look for tungsten. Walter showed him our scintillator, and suddenly he became serious.

A prospector is just what the word implies. He lives with chance, like a gambler. This one led us into, back, and over impossible terrain with all the agility of a mountain goat. We worked one old shaft after another. Nightfall, and the temperatures dropped below freezing. Walter and I huddled in our sleeping bags. The old mountain man was still outside the tent, staring into the campfire, drinking coffee laced with whiskey. Somewhere, a timber wolf howled. The tent flaps parted and the old man crawled inside. He took off his boots and it was more than I could bear.

"Jeezus, brother! You gotta put those things outside!"

Rancid was too mild a word to describe the smell coming from the inside of those boots. He laughed and told me he had never known a sick day in all his 75 years. The secret to good health, in his opinion, was to stay out of the water.

"Water's for drinking, and if God had meant us to immerse our bodies in the stuff, he would've given us gills. Damn water opens your pores and lets in disease!"

"You mean you ain't never had a bath?" Walter asked.

"Not in the last 25 years, as I can remember." He put his boots outside, pulled a blanket over himself, and began to snore like a band saw.

Minutes seemed like hours, and another snoring noise began to harmonize with those coming out of the old man— only these sounds were outside the tent. I rose up and peeked through a crack in the canvas. A huge bear was inspecting our tent. I reached for the rifle my brother and I had placed between us and knew that if that bear poked his nose into our tent, I was going to blast him. It never came to pass. The bear took one sniff of those boots, shook his head, and went on his way.

It was almost sundown the next day when we finally got back to the old man's cabin. The search had been fruitless and Walter and I had had our fill of prospecting. The old man suggested we spend one more night in our tent before attempting the hazardous road that led back to town. He closed the door on his cabin and returned to his private world.

The next morning, there was a bright new pickup truck parked in front of the cabin. How it got there, I will never know. Walter and I had slept like dead men that night. What followed next, I couldn't believe: this good-looking gal—she couldn't have been more than 30—came walking out of the cabin, hand in hand with the dirty old man. She kissed him good-bye long and hard, got into the cab of the truck, and drove away.

"Hey! Old man!" I said, waving a friendly good morning. "You never told us about this part of mining!"

"I get my goodies now and then," he answered with a smile, then turned and went back to his cabin.

Chapter 20

Back home again, sitting with the guys on Waikiki Beach, looking west, trying to see for 2,000 miles.

"Gonna make da bigges' wave you've evah seen."

"Hey bruddah, give me a match. I want to put some moah smoke on dese lenses." Raucous laughter.

This was the day the hydrogen bomb was set to go off on Elugelab Atoll in the Marshall Islands. The radio and newspapers had been full of reports on the awesomeness of this upcoming event. Some tourists and locals alike had misgivings about Hawaii's proximity to the test site, a well-founded concern as we now know. Our little mock display was for their benefit as well as our own. If life wasn't a joke, what was it?

"How they gonna make an explosion be dis big?"

"They make it out of dis kine rock."

"C'mon, you don't make no bomb out of rocks."

"It's what's in da rocks, you dummy. Special powah called 'uranium'."

A bomb went off, all right. Sooner than I expected.

Two neatly-dressed gentlemen in lightweight business suits approached our little circle of merry men. One of them spoke directly to me. "Barry Napoleon?"

"That's me. What can I do you out of?" Laughter all around.

"Hey, Nap, don't that guy owe you some money?"

This time the man didn't wait for the laugh reaction. He reached into his vest pocket and pulled out a small leather billfold, and flashed his credentials in front of my face. I can't remember his name, but I'll never forget his employer's: the Federal Bureau of Investigation.

"I'm Mr. Johnson and this is Mr. Taylor. We're from the Federal Bureau of Investigation. You are under arrest."

"What the hell for?"

"Draft evasion."

• • •

Tiny grains of sand kept dropping off my bare feet and onto the highly polished floor of the Provost Marshall's office in the downtown induction center. I sat in a chair, all alone, listening to every tick of the clock from 10:00 a.m. to 2:00 p.m. It was like a Chinese water torture. *Would they throw me in the Oahu Prison?* I knew guys that had been in there. An awful place. *Was evasion like desertion? Could they shoot you?*

Shortly after 2:00 p.m., the FBI agent entered the room, introduced himself, and pulled down the shade.

"Is it your intention to avoid the draft?"

"No."

"You received your induction notice?"

"I've been movin' around a lot."

"Where have you been?"

"L.A., Utah…all over the place."

"You never thought to apprise the draft board of your whereabouts?"

"No."

"Then it is not your intention to avoid the draft?"

"No."

"Good! Report back here tomorrow at 0800 hours and you will be taken to Schofield Barracks. Welcome aboard!"

The next morning, an army band was playing *The Monkey Wrapped His Tail Around The Flagpole*. The mayor made a short speech. Parents and friends brought flower leis. There were tears and proud farewells. They packed us into a couple of large buses and we were off to Schofield.

• • •

Schofield Barracks was the place Burt Lancaster, Montgomery Clift, and Frank Sinatra made famous in the movie *From Here to Eternity*. The title meant nothing to me when I saw the picture, but now it seemed very significant. We were issued bedding, told to listen for chow call, and to be prepared for tomorrow. Revielle would be at 0500.

That night, Ben Chun, an old friend of mine, organized a big crap game. Nothing new for Ben. He was a big gambler. We had played a lot of dice together in the past and against some pretty high rollers. He let me know the fix. At the end of the night, we split over $3,000.

• • •

The doctor had on a white coat. The sergeant had a clipboard and a pencil. Fifty draftees stood in line without a stitch of clothes. "Bend over and spread your cheeks." The doctor and the sergeant began their tour of inspection. I couldn't stand it. The whole scene was too absurd. As they came up behind me, I bellowed, "What do you see up there, Doc?" The parade stopped.

"Step out of line, soldier! I'll show you what I see."

Forty-nine assholes later, I was ready for the infirmary.

• • •

We assembled in a big room to be officially sworn in. The top brass eyed this disheveled group with practiced disdain. A captain stepped forward. The sergeant yelled "TAINHUT!"

The captain said, "Any announcements, Sergeant?" The sergeant looked down at his clipboard. "The following men will not be accepted in the Army of the United States."

The first name to be read was mine. The old football injuries—the busted knee and the torn shoulder—had not been in vain. I left all my clothes and took a cab back to Waikiki with some $1,500 in my pocket.

Chapter 21

By the end of the week, I was broke, but not disheartened. I did a lot of women, drank a lot of wine, ate like a king, and stayed in the finest hotels. But, best of all, I landed a job on the beach at Waikiki.

The Surfrider Hotel was the tallest building in Waikiki, and Kalakaua Avenue was an uncrowded two-way street. The old International Market Place, the highrise hotels, were but unfertilized seeds lying dormant in the minds of real estate developers more concerned with the outcome of the Korean War than the economic potential of a small stretch of beach known as Waikiki. An old Ford Woody wagon loaded with fresh-cut flowers was always parked in front of the Outrigger Canoe Club. Hawaiian ladies wearing coconut hats sat on campstools by the open doors, weaving their leis, playing ukuleles, and greeting passersby.

There were two beach concessions on Waikiki at the time: Earl Akana's Hale Au Au, which was located on the Diamond Head side of Waikiki, and the Outrigger Canoe Club, which was sandwiched next to the Royal Hawaiian Hotel. The Outrigger was staffed by the old-time beach boys that rode into prominence with the exploits of Duke Kahanamoku—the kind of guys that made up the background for the old Bing Crosby movies. *Sweet Leilani*, coconut hats, and ukuleles. Names like Panama Dave, Chick Daniels, Turkey Love, and Steamboat. Hawaii was, at best, a dream for most mainlanders in those days, and the Outrigger, in conjunction with the Royal Hawaiian, did its best to see that these beach boys maintained an aura to best fulfill the dreams of the few well-heeled tourists who could visit our Islands and carry back their pictures and stories to friends and relatives and start the economic tourist ball rolling.

Hale Au Au catered to the newer wave of tourists finding its way to Hawaii's shores. Our boys were a generation removed from the Outrigger prototypes—an elite crew of strong, capable young watermen schooled all our lives on the beaches of Oahu: Bobby Krewson, Ed "Blackout" Whaley, Mud Werner, Buckshot Stanford, Buddy Kahanamoku—all the sons of Kalakaua. The sun was our time clock, and before the average tourist had opened his or her eyes in the morning, we had the beaches swept and raked clean, the canoes lined up and pointed towards the sea, and the rental surfboards in their racks. Surf and sea conditions were checked and tested firsthand, for this was our playtime. Long before the first imprint of a beach-goer's foot was made in the sand, we had surfed our waves, been sun-dried, and recounted last night's adventures over steaming mugs of good strong coffee.

• • •

Waikiki Beach, our sleeping lady, was now awake. People were laying down their mats. The aroma of suntan lotion filled the air. An artist was setting up his easel and rustling through his bag for paints and brushes. Let me tell you what he saw: a weather-beaten, two-story structure stood between the Royal Hawaiian and the Outrigger Canoe Club. It was nestled among palm trees, and the grounds were overgrown with lush vegetation. Countless layers of paint covered the redwood sidings; this year it was green, but tell-tale chips and cracks revealed veins of whites, yellows and blues from seasons past. The locals would say that the entire building was held together by rusty nails and the spirit of aloha. They called it the "old ladies' home." The shaded veranda looked out over a picture-book marine scene—the smell of the South Seas in the air. A sleek canoe, carved from native koa wood, filled with happy faces and a high-riding steersman, could be seen racing a blue-green wave frothing with foam. Tan, graceful surfers rode long, wooden surfboards, and the white cotton sail of a catamaran embossed with a bluebird flapped defiantly against the trade winds in an effort to free its two beached hulls from the clutches of the sticky, wet sand composed of ground-up seashells. A narrow, splintered walkway led to the beach. Off to the right the Halekulani Hotel, its thatched-roof bungalows protected by a sea wall, marked the beginning of Waikiki Beach. To the left, the Moana and Surfrider Hotels guarded Kalakaua Avenue from the encroaching high tide. Diamond Head loomed majestically in the background.

    A clear, falsetto voice accompanied by soft guitars echoed off the water. It was Saturday afternoon and a crowd had gathered beneath the big banyan tree on the terrace of the

Moana to watch Webley Edwards conduct the radio show Hawaii Calls. Al Kealoha Perry stood in front of his musicians. The voices of Alfred Apaka and Bonnie Isaacs blended with the sounds of steel guitars, and their music floated out across the water to mix with the rhythm of the waves.

Directly in front of the Moana was a break we called Baby Canoes. Beginners got their first surfing lessons there. The water was shallow, at times no more than waist deep. We were able to stand and push our pupils into the waves. Outside, there were bigger waves. This was known as Canoes. Every picture of a surfing canoe adorning the face of a travel poster was taken there.

Standing on the beach and looking out 100 yards to the left, surfers could be seen sliding right across the face of Queens. At one time, a wooden pier extended out into the water here. It was built especially for the Queen, and her surfboard was always kept in readiness. When the waves came up to suit her fancy, she would walk out over the water, paddle a mere 50 yards and go surfing.

Populars was located in front of the Royal Hawaiian, so-called because it was the most unpopular place to go surfing at Waikiki. Razor-sharp coral heads lurked just beneath the surface. A wipeout could result in nasty cuts that would take weeks to heal. As more and more tourists began to venture out into the water, a demolition team was brought in to blast out the coral.

Continuing down the beach, the shoreline got smaller. Beach-walkers would slosh through the tidal advances and sunbathers would retreat to the sanctuary of the warm sea wall. The Hale Au Au concession stood in the shadow of the Surfrider.

The beach boys would wait for customers to sign up for board rentals, surfing lessons, and canoe rides. Hamburgers sizzled on an outdoor charcoal pit as *malahinis* and *kamaainas* circled ever so slowly around the hau-covered terrace of the Merry-Go-Round Bar, beachside of the old Waikiki Tavern. Calls for Mai Tais and Primo beer blended with merry voices and raucous laughter. Mynah birds perched on the railing impatiently waiting for handouts and opportune moments to steal leftovers from vacant tables.

    The last building on the row, a two-story structure known as the Waikiki Sands, rested on pilings bent by time and tide. It was the home of the Waikiki Surf Club and a restaurant that served the best buffet lunch in the Pacific: lau lau, lomi salmon, poi, sushi, tofu, chop suey, exotic fruits, salad, steak, lobster, shrimp and crab. The bill of fare was as endless as the appetites. "All You Can Eat," the sign said, "$1.50." Small, inexpensive apartments were available on the second floor and at night, when the tide was high, the whole place seemed to come alive. It swayed to the undulating motions of the sea and pulsated to the bumps and grinds of the strippers cavorting in the Orchid Room on the top floor.

    An alleyway led to the sidewalk and Kalakaua Avenue. Wally Young's store measured no more than 20 by 20. He sold everything from mysterious Oriental elixirs to fresh peaches. Inside, there wasn't a square inch of available space that was not put to work. Groceries and produce were stacked to the ceiling and shoppers had to make their way through a maze of narrow passages. There was no way of telling how old some of the merchandise at the floor level was, for selections were always made from the top or the whole design would have collapsed.

Mud Werner and I were eating a 65¢ special: char siu and rice, with a paper cup brim-full of macaroni salad. "Mud," I asked. "If you had all the money in the world and could buy anything in that store you wanted, what would you get?"

"A great big jar of Best Foods mayonnaise," was the immediate and unpremeditated reply.

Mud was an old friend, and I'd grown used to answers like that. Guess that's why I asked him questions. A powerfully built man, he was a canoe captain for Hale Au Au. All the beach boys at Hale Au Au were in their 20s—strong watermen and ready for anything. They had to be. That's where the action was.

Chapter 22

His mother was Spanish, his father was English, and he was all Kanaka. He'd been on the beach every day as long as I had, and his name was Bobby Krewson. He was far and away the sharpest guy that had ever worked the sands. His repeat clientele included such names as Tony Martin, Cyd Charisse, Buddy Adler, Rory Calhoun, Abbott and Costello, Gene Shacove, and many others too numerous to mention.

One day, Bobby picked up a little Haole girl off the beach at Makaha, took her out in the water, and won the tandem surfing competition.

• • •

Hoot! Hoot! The Matsonia blasted its warning signal. The noise reverberated around the harbor. "All ashore that're going ashore!" shouted the ship's steward as he made his way down the passageway of B Deck.

In a small cabin, secreted behind the closed doors, Bobby Krewson and I were saying last passionate good-byes to a couple of luscious honeys from San Francisco. The girls were dressed in their best traveling clothes, and we were doing our best to mess them up. Bobby and I were wearing semi-clean white cotton shorts and aloha shirts.

"I don't know about you, brah," I say to Bobby, "but I ain't goin' back. I'm stowing away to San Francisco with this chick!"

"Me, too! We can get jobs over there, *mebbe* stay a couple of years. Three, if you like!"

The girls look at each other as if to say, *Now, fun is fun, but this is going too far.* "You can't be serious! You just can't! Can you?"

I move away from my girl and flop down on the bed, resting my head on the interlaced fingers of my hands. Bobby follows suit on the other bed, leaving both girls bewildered in the middle of the room.

"Dis is da life, eh, brah?"

The Matsonia sounded its final warning, and the girls panicked.

"You guys have got to get out of here! Now!"

"*Whatsa matta?* You don't think we do too good in San Francisco?"

The boat began to vibrate. One of the girls rushed to the porthole.

"My God! We're leaving!"

Bobby started singing and dancing the hula around the room. The girls immediately started losing their hard-earned summer tans and turned white as ghosts.

"Hey, let's order some food down *heah*," I said.

"Naw," Bobby answered. "Take too long. We can sneak it out of the kitchen. *Mebbe* some beer, too, eh?"

"I knew these girls didn't want you just for your body! You

got a head on your shoulders, brah!"

We bolted from the cabin, leaving two blonde heads staring in disbelief out of the portholes as the ship headed for the open sea. In a loud voice from just outside the open stateroom door, Bobby piped up: "Hey, brah! We forgot the *wahines*! They gotta help us!"

I re-entered the room, whisked the two near panic-striken girls away from their portholes, and off we went. The fun was just beginning.

Bobby and I laughed like two crazy men at the little joke we'd worked so many times before. A ship's officer approached from the stern. We buried ourselves in the crowd that had gathered on the upper deck to savor one last look at the mountains and shores of Oahu. Cameras clicked away and tearful tourists threw flowered leis into the sea. Whitecaps rode atop wind-blown swells. The ship had worked its way some five miles off Waikiki and, up ahead, like a proud lady in waiting, is the Hale Au Au canoe. Her crew, composed of Blackout, Mud, Buddy Kahanamoku, and Buckshot, waved their paddles in last alohas.

The time came. We climbed the ship's rail, balanced for a moment, waved good-bye to the two girls, and dove like seabirds into the churning blue.

A monster ship the size of the Matsonia creates a tremendous suction, and unless extreme caution is exercised, one could easily be pulled back under the hull and torn apart by the spinning propellers. We surfaced and fought through the deadly currents to the canoe. The ship's wake was covered with leis, a symbolic salute to another short piece of time gone from our lives.

Chapter 23

The Huddle Restaurant was little more than a shack carved into the corner of the arcade building. It sat right on the beach, backed up against the wall of the Surfrider. The owner's name was Lau, and the beach boys were his bread and butter. Lau never bothered to sweep out the diner. Instead, he raked it from time to time. After a busy day, the floor would be covered with sand and littered with cigarette butts. About every six months, he would have the sand changed because, as he explained it, things would get to the stage where raking just wasn't good enough. He opened at sunrise and closed at sundown, and I don't believe there was a light in the place.

Breakfasts at the Huddle were special. In the early mornings, we would lay our nets and take the catch back to Lau. He would cook the fish of our choice and only charge us for the rice he served on the side. Most always, there was enough seafood left over to see him through an entire day.

The beach boys laid claim to their own special territory in the Huddle, and at least one of us was always on hand to see that our private domain was protected. Our table stood next to the window facing the sea. This particular spot afforded a perfect view of the beach in front of the Surfrider. Pretty girls were sized up and prospective paying clients were analyzed. It reminded me of laying and waiting behind a duck blind.

• • •

The sun had not been up a full hour yet. Bobby, Mud, Buckshot, and some guy I'd never seen before had the big canoe jam-packed full of diving gear and were just about ready to shove off into the ocean. I ran as fast as I could, peeling off my pants and shirt, shouting, "Hey! You guys! Wait up!"

"Hurry up, Nap! Go get your gear!"

I turned right around and ran back the other way. Diving was always exciting. I tossed my fins, mask and spear on the pile and jumped into the boat.

"Hey, Nap!" Bobby yelled from behind me once we were underway in the canoe. "That guy sittin' in front of you there is Freddy Noa. He's here with the roller derby."

Freddy turned and nodded, and I did the same, saying, "Howzit?"

"Okay," he answered.

Freddy was about my age, broad shoulders, looked like he'd been a paddler all his life. I thought I knew most everybody on the Island, but I couldn't seem to place him.

"Hey, you from Kalihi?" I half-shouted as we paddled out beyond the surf line.

"Chicago," he yelled back, never turning his head around.

"Yeah, I know that. Your team is on tour, but…where were you born?"

"Chicago. Born and raised. My old man moved there a long time ago."

We got out in the water and the guy became a seal. He dove as good as anybody I'd ever seen before. Back on shore he gave us his catch, and told us to be sure and come to the derby that night. He'd leave some tickets for us at the window.

Freddy Noa's job may have afforded the opportunity to see the world, but what a heck of a way to make a buck! Guys flew around the board track, kicking the hell out of each other. Freddy was a tiger—a real crowd pleaser. How he lived through the night, I will never know.

After it was over, we all met for something to eat. Freddy was calm, collected, and wanted to know if we could go diving again. We took him surfing instead. He had never been on a surfboard before. As we sat off Queens on our boards and he made one fruitless attempt after another to catch a wave, I asked him, "How come you can dive so good and don't know how to surf?"

"Spent a lot of time in Florida during the off season."

Another wave came and this time Freddy was off flying. He was a natural.

Freddy played out his contract and returned to Honolulu to stay. Within four months, he was riding the big winter waves at Makaha. He rented a small house at Kawela Bay, went skin diving all day, threw parties all night.

Freddy was a nice dresser. He had an air of authority about him, which made him look more like the owner than a manager. Freddy later became the assistant manager of the Tradewind Restaurant. He called me late one night from the bar and said he was stuck there all alone and having a hell of a time with some pretty good-sized *haole* guys, backed up by one Kanaka. Could I come down and give him a hand? I was only a few minutes away, so I jumped out of bed and got dressed.

When I arrived, Freddy was waiting for me at the entrance.

"What's the trouble, brah?" I asked.

"Aw, there's four of 'em, real trouble-makers. They're breaking glasses, swearing, threatening to walk the check."

Freddy led me inside and we walked right into them. They walked out the door and the bill was still on the table, beer-soaked and crumpled.

"Hey, wait a minute," Fred yelled. "You've got a $40 tab here."

The biggest guy turned, crumpled up two $20 bills, and threw them at Fred. Fred reached down, picked up the two bills and caught up to thief just outside the door.

"You little Kanaka! I'm going to have me a piece of your ass 'fore this night's over."

"I'd like to see that," Fred said. "How's the parking lot sound?"

We lined up beside the parked cars, four looking at two.

"Here I am, pal.. You want a piece of my ass?"

The guy moved toward Freddy, and that was all he did. Freddy whaled on him. One of the other guys started to go after Fred, and I stepped in between. "Hey, pal, this is not your beef. If you think so, you're going to deal with me."

The account was settled and Fred and I went back to the bar.

"You know, Nap?" he said. "That was kind of fun, just like the roller derby."

Chapter 24

Rabbit Kekai, Jamma, Nigger Dan, and Samson were brothers. They grew up on Waikiki Beach. Rabbit was by far the best surfer the waves have ever produced at that time; no one won more surfing contests and tandem competitions than he did. Jamma liked to sail; there was never enough wind for him, so we likened him to a windjammer, or "Jamma" for short. Nigger Dan was the darkest of the brothers, and Samson the strongest. Rabbit was still active on the beach long after the others had retired and gone, and I never passed his surfboard stand without thinking of those wonderful days when the beach meant more than a buck.

• • •

The courtyard of the Moana Hotel was filled with people. The crowd spilled over on the beach. The first annual coconut tree climb was about to start. Contestants nervously waited their turns in line. The tree was 25 feet high and Rabbit set a record that day that will live forever. No one has ever even come close to breaking his time, for the following year, in the second annual contest, the tree had grown to 35 feet high.

• • •

Friday night. First View, the weekly big movie premier at the Waikiki theater, wouldn't start until ten o'clock. There was plenty of time. Rumors were flying around Waikiki Beach that Buzzy Trent had put nothing in his stomach for two days but water—gallons and gallons of water. Tonight, he was going for the record.

M's Ranch, a steakhouse out on Kalanaianaole Highway between Kahala and Aina Haina, had a come-on gimmick under the guise of a contest. The only opponent: a menu and a clock. Conquer them both, and it was a free dinner, compliments of the house. The bill of fare consisted of a bowl of soup, tossed green salad with choice of dressing, one baked potato loaded with sour cream and chives, a fresh vegetable, a 64-ounce steak, a dinner-size loaf of bread with four pats of butter, pie à la mode, and a beverage of the contestant's choice. At the end, nothing, save the steak bone, could remain in any form on the plate.

Now, all this was free if one could do it in less than 25 minutes. Bud Browne, one of the original surf film makers, was on hand with lights and camera. He had a contingent of California surfers with him, two of whom were entries. Pat Curren, another guy from California, had entered unattached—no sponsor. If he lost, he'd pay. Pat hadn't eaten for a day, simply because he hadn't had anything to eat. Pat lived out of the back of his car with a surfboard for a bed partner.

Buzzy Trent was one of the first of a wave of California surfers to come to our Islands, along with this same Pat Curren, Dale Velzy, Mike Diffenderfer, and Joe Quigg. The first day Buzzy surfed Makaha, we knew he was for real. He took on waves of monstrous size with reckless abandon. These guys were special in that they were eager to learn Hawaiian ways and they respected them. They lived out in the country, mostly for two reasons: they were here to surf, and they were on extremely meager budgets.

I remember Pat Curren forcing his old junker car around Kaena Point and testing himself off the beaches of Sunset, Waimea, and Laniakea. Big wave boards were long and narrow, had pointed tails—"big guns," they were called; it was down the face and go for broke.

The cameras rolled all the time, carrying films back to mainland surfers who had never dreamed of waves like these. The word got out, and the mass surfer invasion began. But these handful of guys I mentioned—the firsts—had a respect for Hawaii, its people, and its ways. They kept pretty much to themselves but never backed off. Pat Curren held his ground one night when a big guy came at him with a knife. It tore through his hand to the bone; he wrapped it up in a rag and was still there long after the guy was gone.

We played music together, taught them songs, went diving, and even followed them to their kind of haunts, like M's Ranch. The record? Oh yeah…Buzzy set a new one that night: 18 minutes! The other two guys had to push away from the table. And Pat Curren hung in there until he got sick.

Chapter 25

One morning, I had just returned to the beach from the Kaiser Hospital where I had deposited one of our board renters who had sustained a nasty gash in his head. As I passed the Huddle, I saw a ruckus going on inside. Some guy had Lau by the neck and was threatening to tear his head off. I pulled the attacker off and flattened him. Lau was able to tell me later, when his larynx relaxed, that the guy had run up a large bill, and when Lau asked for a payment, it almost cost him his life. From that day on, I always enjoyed carte blanche at the Huddle. Lau never allowed me to pay for anything.

We took great pride in the beach. It was our home. By 8:00 a.m., the sand was raked clean, the boats lined up at the water's edge, and the surfboards ready in their racks. We surfed until people began to appear, carrying their beach mats, towels, and endless varieties of suntan lotion. Today was our future.

• • •

The beach boys had their own coconut wireless. We knew who was staying where, when someone was due to arrive, and how long they would be in Waikiki. When a lone woman came on the beach at the Royal Hawaiian Hotel, you could bet she was no stranger to us—particularly if she was a bit past her prime. Ladies like this could be the most fun of all. You learned to read her walk, her attire, her every mannerism; and the gleam in her eyes—the one we called the sexual "come here." Time, for once, becomes an ally. You know it's too precious for her to waste.

A quick stop at the beach desk and you come away with enough information to start and hold a conversation. Could anything possibly be more flattering than to have a well-built, bronzed beach boy approach and ask in a deep, intimate tone, "Would you like to take a surfboard ride?" Forget about propriety. Here you are, in the area of 50, one side or the other, on the beach and in a bathing suit. Even the thought that he thinks you can do it can turn back the mental clock 20, maybe 30 years. Nine times out of ten her answer will be no, why ruin a good thing. So you sit down and begin to "talk story" with her.

"I've seen you on the beach before. I bet you must come here every year."

"Ever since 1946. My husband and I have fallen in love with this place."

"How long are you planning to stay with us?" I ask.

"Ten days. At least that's our plan."

"Then you don't want to take any chances and spoil your time. I noticed your back is getting a little red. Hawaiian sun is very strong."

You pick up the bottle of suntan lotion that lies atop every towel. "May I?" you ask.

"Why, thank you."

The reply contains a slight self-conscious air. The cap comes off the bottle and you cover that hard to reach bare place on her back with what we call "sexy stroke": forward and back at the same time. It's nothing really but the old Hawaiian *lomi lomi* technique. A physical contact is made here, one that doesn't happen at the home-town country club. The ice is broken, her hair is down, you've made a friend, and she accepts the offer of a canoe ride. Hell, anybody can look good riding in a canoe.

The salt water has washed away the suntan lotion, and she's all smiles when you set her up for the rest of the sunny day by a last, quick 'sexy stroke' application. This usually ends in a thank you and a healthy tip, but not before she has dropped a few confidential remarks on you—the kind any hair stylist only too willingly repeats. You tell her it's time to get back to work. You've enjoyed being with her, and—oh, one other thing: if she'd like a *lomi lomi* after the beach, you'll be free between two and three. All you need is her room number.

That's the way we played it and that's the way it worked. If the number was forthcoming, you knew you were in. Ladies like these lived most of their lives according to rules. The thought suddenly strikes her that now, for the first time, she has broken one, but isn't sure.

"This is all right with the management, isn't it? I mean, you coming up to my room and all?"

"Of course. We do it all the time."

A little-girl like veil of naughtiness comes over her. Now, the beach boys were not allowed above the first floor after 6:00 in the evening, but that's your worry. Take the back stairs.

The employees are your friends. You knock gently on the door, holding a small bag containing coconut oil mixed with olive oil. Every woman is different. You know that. How she may react to this, well, you know that, too. But initially, all you're there for is to pick up some bucks by giving a good *lomi lomi*.

• • •

Today, the door opened and she's wearing a bathrobe. I enter the room and she's very nervous. My moves must be cautious and low key, my voice gentle and friendly.

"Hello, there. All ready for the big operation?"

"I guess so. What am I supposed to do?"

In a very professional manner, I put my bag down and turned back the covers on the bed. "You just relax. That's the important thing. Now, I'm going into the bathroom to wash my hands. While I'm gone, take off your robe, get under the sheet, and lie down on your *opu*—I mean, stomach."

"God, if the Women's Club could see me now!"

"Not to worry. You're in good hands."

She's in position by the time I re-enter the room. "All comfortable?" I ask.

"Quite, thank you."

"That's good. Now I want you to close your eyes, rest your head on the pillow, and just relax. I promise, this won't hurt a bit."

"You sound just like my dentist back home."

"He gives *lomi lomi*, too?"

"No, my dear. Far from it."

I straddle her *okole*, resting on my knees, allowing just a hint of contact. I pull the sheet back over her shoulder and pour a mixture in my hands and start with the neck and shoulders. My thumbs follow the line down each side of her spine, hands working the muscles on the left and right sides. This procedure follows all the way down to the small of the back, but never baring her bottom. Her muscles and your hands communicate, they instruct, they tell you things you would never be able to utter. In this instance, the reading is clear: please continue.

I'm straddling her thighs, now, the covers pulled down. There's nothing more pleasant to a woman than to feel a man kneading her rump. I've gone far enough. It's time to cover her up. The sheet comes up from the bottom and I start on her feet. Feet say many things, and by the time you reach a point just above the knee the signs become bell clear. The thighs begin to pull away from each other. Down comes the sheet. I turn her over and start with the feet once again. The sheet stays down this time. I work underneath, pushing upward. When you're squatting just over her knees, your hands are about to touch home base. All motion stops, *lomi lomi* is over.

I start to get up. "Well, that's it for today."

They're all different. Every last one. I've had hands reach up under my trunks. "You can't go now. I want you."

"But if the hotel ever found out about a thing like this happening, I'd be in hot water!" (That's a laugh. If the hotel even knew I was above the first floor, all hell would break loose!)

Sometimes it was, "Thank you, that'll be ten dollars, please." I'd head for the john to wash my hands, and as I was putting away my oils I'd have a twenty, sometimes more, and a good customer for the duration of her stay.

One lady, a recording executive from the mainland—she must have been close to fifty—approached me one day in front of the Halekulani.

"You know, my girlfriend told me you give real Hawaiian *lomi lomis*."

She mentioned the girlfriend's name and I drew a blank, but countered with, "Oh, yes, and how is Mildred?"

This lady ripped the sheet right off. "Look at me. Look at me! Am I voluptuous enough for you?"

"Yeah, yeah, you are!"

And she came back every year.

Chapter 26

I looked at my watch. It was 10:30 and I headed for the Huddle to pick up some coffee.

"Excuse me. Can you tell me where the Waikiki Pharmacy is?"

She was the foxiest looking chick I'd ever seen. Her hair was red as fire, her skin milky white. A kelley-green jumpsuit clung to her body like glue. She had on a big, floopy white hat, sunglasses, and white sandals.

"The Waikiki Pharmacy? What a coincidence! I was just heading there myself."

We took off down Kalakaua Avenue. I was wearing a t-shirt and a pair of trunks, and she looked like she just stepped out of the front cover of a Las Vegas visitors' magazine.

"Where are you staying?" I asked.

"Well, I just moved into a darling little apartment over on Prince Edward Street," she answered.

"Oh, then you're planning to be here a while."

"Just a couple of weeks, but I like the privacy of an

apartment. Would you like to see it? It's a great party pad. Do you like parties?"

"Huh! I live for parties!" I replied, almost walking into a palm tree.

"How divine. Maybe you could help me throw one? What do you call them? *Loouhs?*"

• • •

Prince Edward Street was like all the other small, narrow thoroughfares in Waikiki that ran between Kalakaua Avenue and the Ala Wai Canal. Small, wooden apartments housing hotel employees, bartenders, musicians, and dancers were sandwiched between inexpensive hotels where the budget-minded tourists in transit could find a room with a shower, an undersized dresser, a nightstand, two lamps, a lumpy bed, and cockroaches.

We walked past a series of palm-shrouded signs—the Surfboard Hotel, the Princess Lanai, Waikiki Paradise, Seaside Inn, and finally, the Prince Edward Apartments. I followed her down a narrow walkway overgrown with hibiscus bushes to a small, ground-level apartment, secreted in the back. She fumbled nervously through an oversized purse for the key and worked it back and forth in the lock to no avail. Our bodies brushed together as I stepped in front of her, gave the key a firm half twist, and popped the door open. With a courtly gesture, I ushered her inside and closed the door.

We stood looking at each other for a brief moment, smiled, touched, and embraced. Jeezus, I thought to myself, this is too much. Her head rested on my shoulder and the smell of her filtered through my nostrils and exploded in my brain.

We moved toward the bed, our hands moving feverishly over shoulders, thighs and okoles. I felt her body stiffen as the sliding zipper on the back of her jumpsuit cut through the silence of the morning air. Nimble fingers found their way to the buttons on the front of my trunks. At moments like this, time and life seem to stand still. It then picks up again, having deposited its passengers in a nebulous world of sensuous delights. We laid down on the bed together and began to make love.

Suddenly, there was a loud knock on the door. We both froze and the knocking stopped. Just as quickly, it started up again, but louder this time, and with more authority.

"Who the hell is that?" I whispered.

"I don't know."

We held on to each other in complete silence. The knocking reverberated through the room like a jackhammer. Man, my *ule* went limp as I turned my head toward the door, expecting an irate husband, the police…my god, who knows who could be out there!

The pounding stopped and the silence was deafening, only to be broken by the sound of padding footsteps retreating back toward the street. Our eyes met, I felt my *ule* grow hard, and our movements carried us to a climactic finish.

As I was leaving, a small clock on the nightstand said Aloha, it's 11:15. Scarcely 45 minutes had passed since I left the beach and started for coffee. I had lived a lifetime.

When I got back to the stand, I was beside myself. What a way to start a morning! I saw Bobby Krewson heading my way.

"Hey, Bobby! Come over here!"

Bobby sauntered across the sand. "Hey, we've been pals a long time."

"I know that," he said. "Whatsa matta with you?"

"Bobby. Bobby, I've never lied to you, have I?"

"Hey, you in trouble or something?"

"Bobby, do I look like I'm in trouble?"

"No," he said.

"Well, listen to this, brah, cuz what I'm gonna tell you, you ain't gonna believe. No more than an hour ago, I wuz walkin' over there to get some coffee and I meet this classy, red-headed chick—whew!—in a green, skin-tight jumpsuit. Man! Reddest hair you ever saw! She even had red pubic hairs! She had boobs sticking out to here and, well, now, she hustles me over to her apartment—"

"Hey, hey, hey...wait a minute," he interrupted. "She doesn't happen to live over on Prince Edward Street, does she?"

"Yeah," I answered, "but how'd you know that?"

"Was there a little clock by the bed that said 'Aloha' on it?"

"Why, you sonovabitch, do you know her?"

"Do I know her? Man, I met her in front of the Moana early this morning! She asked me if I knew of any apartments for rent. I took her over to Billy Cross's mother's place on Prince Edward Street, she gave the manager two weeks' worth of rent, and we went to her room. Man, I gave her a quick screw!"

"You're kiddin' me!" I said. "Why, I just got through screwin' her!"

Bobby laughed till he almost fell down. "Hey, hey, hey! We're brothers now, eh, Nap?"

No sooner had we recovered then Freddy Noa comes down to the beach.

"Howz it, brah," he says. "Hey, Bobby, what's doing?"

Freddy's face was all lit up like he just got through opening up a Christmas present.

"Hey, what's up, Freddy?"

"Oh, I think I'll just go take a paddle out in the ocean, relax a little bit. My day was already made."

"Hey, you braggin', huh? Or complainin'?"

"I'm bragging. I just made love to the best-looking red-headed chick you ever saw in your life!"

Bobby and I look at each other. He started to tell us about this girl he had run into at the Waikiki Pharmacy, how he had made a date with her, and the feeling of disappointment that came over him when he knocked on her door and she wasn't home.

"It only goes to show you, brah, all good things come to he who waits, cuz when I got back there, this..."

"Hey, hey, hey, Freddy, hold it right there, brah," I said, unable to contain myself any longer. "Does she live over there on Prince Edward Street?"

"How'd you know that?"

"And there's this clock next to her bed, says 'Aloha' on it?"

"Do you know her?"

"Do I know her? When you were knocking on her door this morning, I was in there screwin' that chick! And you know who screwed her before I did? Bobby! She just arrived here this morning, it ain't even one o'clock yet, and we've all three screwed her!"

Chapter 27

Waikiki night lights. Smoke from charcoal broilers, milling people, and restaurants made to look like sea shanties. Bamboo nightclubs with 8" x 10" black and white glossy photos out in front, featuring entertainers inside—names like Jesse Kalima, Martin Denny, Jules Ah See, and Hau Nani, their voices and instruments clearly audible on Kalakaua Avenue. Sailors from His Majesty's Royal Navy stood on street corners, and a party of white dinner-jacketed tourists could be seen leaving the grounds of the Royal Hawaiian, bound for Don the Beachcomber's. One of the elegantly-clad ladies stood apart from all the rest. She had flaming red hair and white skin.

"Betty Boop" was a divorcee from California. Like so many others who had become disenchanted with the rigors of the eight-to-five routine, Friday afternoon happy hours, the occasional two week romance that ends in a motel room, she came to Hawaii in search of a dream. For many, the dream comes to an end when the money runs out and/or a broken romance leaves yet another scar on a too-eager heart. Betty

Boop, however, saw a potential nightmare turn into a real-life fantasy.

Betty met Mud on the beach. It was a whirlwind affair. They used to get up off the beach and into the basement of the Hale Au Au locker room, at which point we used to sneak around in back, crawl through the basement window, and spy on them. Pants would come down, Mud would lean her up against the wall, and away they'd go. I often wondered if he suspected anything was up, especially when they would walk back out on the beach and there were no beach boys around.

One day, Bobby came up to me. "Hey, Nap! You hear da news?"

"What news you talkin' about, Bobby?"

"Da kine Mud news. He's gettin' married."

"You're kiddin'! To who?"

"To Betty Boop!"

Poor Betty Boop was pregnant and Mud had just enough money to buy dinner. A cheap dinner. A little while later, Mud came over to me and told me he was going to get married, that he'd gotten Betty Boop *hapai*.

"You know, Nap, I owe her something," he said, dejectedly.

"I wish I had all kinds of money. I'd throw her the biggest wedding you ever saw. Hey! Would ya like to help me get a little something together? Invite all the beach boys da kine stuff?"

"Sure, Mud. We can work together on this thing. When are you planning to get married?"

"Fast. I tink dis Friday."

"Friday? It's already Monday! We gotta do something quick!"

Herb Bessa and Woody Brown ran the catamarans. I asked

them how they felt about taking Friday off and playing a part in Mud's wedding, using their boats. Anything they could do for Mud, they would do, they said. I called all the beach boys together, and in no more than 30 minutes, the wedding was planned.

Late Friday morning, Bessa and Woody were waiting with their catamarans in front of the Halekulani. Mud was escorted aboard one of the boats, wearing a red cape and *malo*. Betty was lifted up on the other, dressed in a gorgeous white sarong. All the canoes on Waikiki Beach were assembled behind them, laden with fresh-picked flowers and fruits of every variety, gifts for Mud and his new bride. The cats took to the water and sailed around the bend to the beach in front of the Outrigger Canoe Club, followed by 20 colorful canoes. Rev. Akaka was waiting on the beach with Papa Brea, the Kahuna. His chants sent chills running down spines. As the bride and groom stepped off the boats and onto the sand, they joined hands. The beach boys, 20 canoefuls, left their boats and formed a procession line, singing *Imi Au Ia Oe*. The voices of Island girls joined those of the boys, and tourists and friends from one end of Waikiki to the other closed in on this Hawaiian wedding scene. The Spirit of Aloha was everywhere, and little Betty Boop became queen for a day.

After the ceremony the celebration began. Musicians set up on the sand, chickens boiled in pots, tapa-covered tablecloths were smothered with lau laus. Cases of champagne began showing up on the beach, gifts from hotel tourists so caught up in what they were seeing they wanted to contribute and play a part. The beach was alive with celebrants until well after midnight.

I wasn't looking forward to the clean-up job in the

morning! Even now, at this late hour, there were things to be put away and attended to before any thought about going home could be entertained. It was after 3:00 a.m. The beach was deserted. I walked down to the water's edge, dead tired, thinking back of what we had done, the haunting strains of *E Miau Miau Oe* still echoing in my brain. Or was it an echo? I turned around. Mud and Betty were sitting alone on the sea wall. He was singing and playing his ukulele.

Chapter 28

There was a guy called Taylor, a Samoan. He was a catamaran captain and used to beach his boat in front of the Outrigger Canoe Club. He had a war-scarred face from a thousand fights and prowled around Waikiki Beach like a six-foot, 245-pound tomcat. Nobody wanted to fool with Taylor, for he was just as tough as he was big. He liked me, though, and if any of the old timers tried to muscle me, Taylor would move right in on them, look 'em straight in the eyes and growl, "Eh! Don't fool around my friend or I'll choke your neck!"

Every day, the hotel tourists would flock around his boat, cash in hand, waiting for the next departure. Taylor never had to solicit rides; in fact, he never talked much at all. He would saunter up the beach, kind of nod, and stand next to me—his cat-like eyes catching every movement in the water and on the shore. Because of his penchant for silence, a lot of people questioned his intelligence, but they were outsiders; the few allowed to penetrate his inner circle knew differently.

What Taylor knew about the sea, he learned from the sea.

We once sailed a catamaran from Waikiki Beach to the Kona Coast on the Big Island of Hawaii in the dead of night, without a compass. Outwardly as rough as a cob, his table manners were above reproach and, with him, a meal was a ritual. It was a beautiful thing just to watch this big guy eat. He approached his food with tenderness and care, and when he had finished eating, there was never a crumb left on his plate. He would fold his napkin and place knife and fork together as though he'd been educated in the finest of European finishing schools. I used to meet him for breakfast occasionally. If we made a date for 7, I'm certain he arrived at 6, for there were always two newspapers—the San Francisco Chronicle and the morning Advertiser—neatly folded and obviously well thumbed next to a pitcher of coffee, well drained. The mask of silence would come off and Taylor would proceed to talk of worldly events.

Taylor never wore shoes. The backs of his heels were as sharp as razor blades, and many is the *wahine* who woke up in the morning after an all-night tussle with Taylor to find the lower half of her sheets cut to ribbons.

I went down to the beach early one morning and found Taylor's catamaran pulled up just beyond the high tide line. The sail was picking up the first movements of the morning breeze. This was not a usual happenstance, as the cats always sailed around from the Ala Wai later on in the day. I went over to investigate and found Taylor under the deck making love to the beautiful *haole* daughter of one of Honolulu's high mucky mucks from the Outrigger Canoe Club. I was flabbergasted.

• • •

Buckshot Sanford had an eye for the ladies and so did

Jewjaw. They were always on the lookout for ways to pick up a few extra bucks so they could live up to their good looks. They started dealing lightly in grass and hashhish, and the inevitable happened. They were busted. The laws were much harsher in those days and, after much dodging and weaving with the authorities, both were put on probation. They weren't supposed to leave the island, or frequent bars.

Now, one afternoon, someone spotted Buckshot and Jewjaw drinking beer in the Blue Room with the rest of the beach boys and reported them. Their probation was revoked. We discovered the identity of the informer. He was a local outcast, trying to ingratiate himself with some kind of authority syndrome at the expense of those he felt had slighted him in some way.

Taylor felt a cowardly act like this perpetrated against our friends and fellow beachworkers could not go unpunished. He called for a meeting in the locker room of the Hale Au Au. And late that night, about 10 of us showed up, out of loyalty to Buckshot and Jewjaw, and a kind of fearful respect for Taylor. But we were hardly prepared for Taylor's plan of reprisal: Leeward Allen, the squealer, must die.

Taylor counted heads and made us draw straws which he had lined up evenly in his ham-like fist. The man ending up with the shortest straw was to, as Taylor so delicately put it, "shoot the rat." It was an awful moment as Taylor offered us a straw, one by one. Afterwards, I always felt that he was dealing from the bottom, that the results of the draw were already fixed in his mind. For he, Samoan Taylor, ended up with the shortest straw.

On the following Friday night, we were to let the air out of Leeward's car in the parking lot of the Biltmore Hotel where he worked in the kitchen. When he came out and discovered the flat and was in the process of removing the tire, Taylor was going to shoot him. Now, because we were already made privy to the scheme, we felt that everyone from the locker room should be at the scene to prevent anyone from ever being able to say anything against anyone, ever.

The days crawled by and finally Friday rolled around. We met shortly after eleven o'clock, deflated the tire, and waited. Leeward came out, never noticed the tire, and started his car. All of us secretly sighed with relief, but it was short-lived; he stopped the car, got out, examined the tire, and opened the trunk. Our hearts stopped. The hub cap clanked to the ground and Taylor made his move. He crossed the parking lot, tapped the unsuspecting Leeward on the shoulder, and put the nose of an Army issue .45 against the temple.

Somewhere, something moved. A bush rustled, and a trash can fell noisily to the ground. I couldn't stand it. I ran up to Taylor. "Quick, man! We gotta get outta here! The vice squad's all over the place!"

Leeward's face was frozen with fear. His eyes widened as he saw the butt end of the gun a split second before it slapped across his face. We scattered in eleven different directions.

Chapter 29

Fingers strummed in unison as flickering flames from the beach fire lit up Buster Jeremiah and our makeshift Hale Au Au quartet, giving ukulele lessons to friends and visitors from across the sea.

> *Test your memory, sweet someone, whoever you might be*
> *Sweet someone, you suit me to a T*
> *Although you pay no attention to me at all*
> *One kiss and, needless to mention, you'd have to fall*

Couples sit in the soft sand, holding hands, sharing the romantic spell of a Waikiki night.

• • •

Earl Akana was a businessman first and a Hawaiian second. He ran a tight ship and was always at the helm. I was naturally quite flattered when he asked me to take charge of the concession for the weekend while he went to Maui. He had about 50 bright red surfboards that had been manufactured on the mainland by Robertson and Sweet. David Sweet was a California surfer with a degree in engineering, and his partner, Cliff Robertson, was a Hollywood actor with an eye for a lucrative investment.

Now, up to that time, I'd spent my working days out in the water, giving surfing lessons and canoe rides, and had never paid much attention to the kind of business volume Akana was doing. The weekend proved to be a real eye-opener. The boards were renting so quick, so fast, that customers were standing in line to pay their money. By the end of the day, at $1 a board, we had grossed over $200 on rentals alone. Canoe rides and lessons were another dimension altogether.

When Earl returned on Monday, I gave him all the receipts and went over the weekend's business with him. He thanked me for a job well done, and I thanked him for the doors he'd opened for me.

"What're you talking about, the doors I've opened for you?"

"Hey, I'm going to open my own business."

He was stunned, and looked upon the bold outburst from a brash kid as an act of defiance, almost an act of hostility.

"Hey, man," I said. "There's room for both of us. A little competition might be a healthy thing. Like the restaurant business. They usually operate on one street and help each other draw."

"Not on this beach! You open up, and I'll run your ass into the ground!"

"Well, you do what you gotta do. I'm going into business for myself and I'll work on my own."

So, I walked out of Hale Au Au and all I had was the shorts I was wearing, a head full of dreams, and I wasn't sure how I was going to put those to work. I walked down past the Surfrider, the Moana, the Outrigger, and wound up in front of the Halekulani, where I ran into a long-time friend, Ralph Soong. I always had a little *aloha* in my heart for Ralph Soong. He was a huge guy, a full-blooded Chinese, who'd been a Ranger in the Second World War. He hated Japanese so bad that when he came back, he kept beating them up at the slightest provocation. A previously mild-mannered man, Ralph put himself through extensive psychiatric treatment so he could rid himself of the demon that was possessing him.

"What're you doing down in this part of the beach, eh, Nap? On a day like this, you should be hustlin' broads over at Hale Au Au, brah."

"I just left Hale Au Au for good. I been thinkin' about going into business for myself. Open my own surfboard stand," I told him.

"Are you kiddin' me? How you gonna do that, brah?"

"I don't know. But this Kanaka's going to find a way."

"Hey, let me give you a piece of advice, brah," he said. "You gotta realize what you're bitin' off heah. This island don't belong to us any more. The *haoles* run everything. They own Akana, they run Outrigger, and you just wait: you gonna see the day they ain't gonna be no space left on this Island for you, for me, 'cept in their puppet shows."

Ralph bought me a hamburger and three for himself, and we used his big tandem board for a backrest while we ate and turned our conversation back to old times and lighthearted frivolity, Hawaiian style. A pretty *wahine* approached us.

"So this is where you hide on your day off?" She was a young chick from Seattle whom I had given a couple of surfing lessons to.

"Hey, I'm not hiding. This is where I live."

"In the Halekulani? Aw, come on."

"Sure. I own this place. And this is Ralph, my Chinese houseboy."

Ralph grinned subserviently and nodded up and down, his two big hands clasped together in obeisance.

"You want to go tandem?" I asked her. "Looks pretty good out there."

"For free?"

I looked her straight in the eye and we both recalled our last time in the water together, the closeness of our bodies, the touchings under the water.

"Sure. For free. This time it's my party. Hey, Ralph, you gonna be usin' your board for a little while?"

"It's yours. I gotta be going to work soon. Keep it for me. I'll come by your place one of these days and pick it up."

· · ·

Her legs were spread in front of me, my chin resting inches from her crotch. She knew it, and she knew I knew she knew it. Her smooth, tan legs pressed against my arms and shoulders, rhythmically paddling up and down, the friction between us lubricated by the warm ocean water. Whitewater loomed up ahead and then covered us in a mantle of foam. Sleep would not come easy that night.

I kept thinking about what Ralph had said, and what the future held in store for me. Then it came to me like a big wave rolling in from the sea. The same hidden force is behind all things, and it's what we do with that force that shapes our destiny. Nobody's gonna own me, not the *haoles* or their hotels. Nobody! I was as free as the waves—to build and build until I reached a climax at the end of my course and finally came crashing down on some far distant, perhaps unknown, shore.

The next day, I loaded Ralph's big board into my old car and headed for the beach. I stood in front of the Moana Hotel in my best pair of trunks and hawked surfing lessons. I caught customers like a fisherman throwing in his line to a school of hungry aku. Before I knew it, I was giving dry land instruction on how to paddle and position yourself on the board, the correct way to stand and fall, and the important ways of staying out of the water and surfacing with the hand raised to avoid injury from high-flying boards.

Next, we were in the water, my pupil paddling and me, my own man, swimming alongside, shouting encouragement and instruction. By the time we reached the surfline, some two hundred yards offshore, my pupil was ready for the real thing. I spent the next hour swimming back and forth, retrieving the board, setting up for the next wave, pushing, shoving, shouting and laughing. Six or seven lessons a day was exhausting work, a hard way to make a buck, but I loved every minute of it and so did my people. That evening, I had thirty water-soaked dollars in the pocket of my trunks.

I met a guy from California on the beach. He was going back to the mainland. He had a nifty balsawood surfboard that he was anxious to sell. The going price for a board like this was $125. We haggled back and forth and settled on $80. I began to collect other boards in much the same manner.

• • •

Bobby Krewson had left Hale Au Au. We drew up a contract in the sand and became partners—a 50/50 ownership in all boards acquired and a 60/40 split on the money that we took in. Bobby was to be responsible for all repairs and maintenance, thus earning a right to the larger portion. In less than a year's time, we owned 75 boards. Our surfboard stand was made out of 2x4s, an A-frame with racks on each side. We put up a small thatch roof to ward off the late afternoon sun and anchored a makeshift desk table in the sand. Wax, paper, pencils and valuables were stored in a small, built-in cabinet. People came to know that everything was safe with us, and they responded with their patronage. We were what we sold—a complete beach service, with one exception: no canoe.

In the early '50s, all the canoes were made from solid koa wood. These things weighed up to 2,000 pounds and it took five or six big guys just to get them in and out of the water. The Outrigger, naturally, had the biggest—a 40-footer called "The Princess." Hale Au Au had one just under 30 feet. These canoes were good money makers, but two things were absolutely necessary to be able to enter into this lucrative part of beach service business: a capable crew, and enough money to put one in the water. We were short on both.

The crew was easy. Blackout was unequivocally the best steersman in the world. Mud and Buster Jeremiah were as good all-around watermen as could be found anywhere. The money for the canoe would take some doing.

Chuck Uyehara was an enterprising Japanese guy who used to hang around the beach in hopes of making contact with good-looking *haole* women. His attempts most usually ended in a short circuit, but he was as persistent as a bird dog, a regular "Mr. Moto Gone Hawaiian." He always wore Sailor Moku pants cut off at the knees. If and when he bent over, his glasses would drop off in the sand, rendering him almost sightless. He threw steak fries nearly every weekend, inviting every available girl on the beach, figuring the law of averages would swing his way and plunge him into a torrid love affair.

Uyehara owned a big koa wood canoe, a phallic symbol if ever there was one. He used it more to impress any *wahines* he could lure up to his house than for fun or profit. What a waste. Every day, Bobby and I would look longingly at it and talk about all the money we could make if only that canoe was ours.

"Let's make him an offer," Bobby said to me.

"With what? We ain't got that kind of money," I said.

"Percentage deal. We'll lease it from him."

"You think he'll go for that?"

"All we got to do is ask," Bobby replied.

Chuck was standing on the steps of the Moana, looking at the girls, when we approached him.

"Hey, Chuck," Bobby said. "Your canoe been doin' nuttin' brother but sittin' under dat coconut tree. It ain't makin' you any money. How 'bout we make da kine deal? We'll give you 10 percent."

"Ten percent? What kind a deal is that?"

"Well, ten percent of something is better than ninety percent of nothin'," Bobby fired back. "You tie up with me and Nappy, you gonna' score more, cuz all da kine *wahines* be comin' around dat canoe."

"Oh, no can do, no can do. Not enough money. I cannot go

for dat."

Bobby turned, looked at me and shrugged his shoulders.

"What the hell," I said. "Give hjm twenty."

"That's too much," he said, and faced Chuck again. "Fifteen percent is our best offer," Bobby said.

"Twenty-five percent," Chuck snapped back, "and the canoe's yours."

"Twenty-five percent? You lousy bugga! Here we're offering you 15 and all the gals you can screw."

"Twenty-five percent."

"You wait here," Bobby said. "Me and my partner got to talk business." We walked down to the water.

"Let's get this show on the road," I said. "We ain't gonna' move him. Give that bastard his 25 percent."

"But that's a real *paké* deal," Bobby said.

"So make it. We ain't makin' any money like this."

We walked back up the beach and Chuck was grinning like a Cheshire cat.

I'd always looked upon Chuck Uyehara as a bit of a buffoon; however, he proved to be a shrewd businessman. We ended up having to give him 25 percent of our gross take. But we had our canoe—the devil with the gross!—and tomorrow was another day.

We packed 'em in. Our profits grew, and Uyehara wanted a bigger cut.

More and more foam surfboards covered with fiberglass began showing up on Waikiki Beach. These boards were lighter, stronger, and impervious to the ravages of salt water. George Downing ordered 100 of these foam boards for the Outrigger Canoe Club. Nobody wanted the balsa wood boards anymore.

They were like aquatic Edsels, and we were stuck with a carload. I reasoned that if the new, lighter boards worked so well, why not a fiberglass canoe? We could make our own. Not only would we have a new first on the beach, we could get out from under Mr. Moto and keep the profits and buy our new boards.

Kenny Choy was a master craftsman in working with fiberglass. Late one night, we went down to the beach and painted Uyehara's canoe with a layer of Wesson oil, then covered it with fiberglass, applied our resin, and pulled off the first mold for an all-fiberglass canoe anywhere.

There is no smell in the world quite like boat resin. To inhale it is to never forget it. It pours like thick syrup and, when mixed with catalyst, hardens like iron. It gets under your fingernails, clogs your pores, sticks to your feet, and ruins your clothes. Kenny and I painstakingly applied thin layers of resin over the sheets of tightly woven fiberglass, working with heat lamps to quicken the hardening process, then sanding and re-sanding to attain perfect form. We left the shop every night and headed straight for the beach. A dip in the cool, dark ocean water was just the thing to cleanse away the fine dust of glass particles that covered our bodies from head to toe.

Our budding craft was guarded with all the secrecy afforded an experimental weapons project. How sleek and beautiful she looked, sitting on the beach that first day. Crowds of onlookers circled her in endless caravans. They were awed by the sight of one man pulling her up and down the beach, alone. Blackout and Mud were ecstatic after their first test ride. They reported that she responded to the touch of a hand and rolled on the surf like velvet. A new dimension had been added to an age-old Hawaiian sport. Uyehara could never figure out how we came up with an exact copy of his canoe, which now sat on the beach collecting salt crust and sand and 25 percent of nothing. Hmm! Who says the Japanese are the greatest copiers in the world!

Chapter 30

I will remember you
Through the cold of the winter night
And should I be ever blue
I'll sing this song of you
Please spare your tears for me, Darling
Smile when I go away
For on this sunny, steamer day
I'll wear your ginger lei

Boat days were special days in a time when a week seemed an hour long. We could see the Lurline coming around Diamond Head, and by the time she reached Steamer Lane, outboards were buzzing towards her like bees to a hive. Tug boats loaded with musicians, dancers, dignitaries, greeting committees, friends and relatives pulled alongside the great white hull, awaiting the splash of her anchors and the captain's first words: "Welcome aboard!"

Songs of old Hawaii filled the air, hula girls bearing leis distributed kisses and *aloha*, while beach boys left their small boats and began diving for coins that showered down from the decks like raindrops from a Kona storm. The strong currents of the open sea would carry the divers the length of the ship to be picked up by the circling outboards and deposited off the bow once again. The relentless force of the incoming tide turned the stern towards the shore. We emerged from the sea and slithered aboard the tugs like sun-drenched dolphins, transforming into half-naked South Sea islanders, scrambling through the ship's companionways to the top decks.

"Aloha! Aloha you all!" Brown bodies wringing wet mingle with awe-struck tourists snapping pictures and accepting familiarities of friendship heretofore unknown to them, save their most intimate moments.

The Lurline would blast her warning signal, the vibration permeating the decks as the giant propellers began to turn anew. The anchor chain would rasp its recall of the heavy hook from the ocean floor. We'd climb the rails, turn back, and wave our last good-byes to the girls before turning to face the rolling sea below. In the next moment, we'd be airborne.

Cabs and buses would be lined up in front of the hotels, discharging visitors. Their baggage would line the streets. When the bags were unpacked and the visitors were settled into their rooms, they'd flock to the beach at Waikiki, and we were there to greet them.

• • •

Panama Dave was under the weather. His age was finally showing. Too many good years of playing and drinking too hard.

"Hey, Nap. Do me a favor, will ya?"

"Name it. You've got it!"

Panama was almost like a father figure to us. Everybody

loved him. Physically, he was a slight man. His face was deeply lined with wrinkles from 65 years of laughter, and I often wondered which came first: the nickname Panama or the big straw hat he always wore.

"Can you handle some kids for me today? It's an all-day thing and, man, I just ain't up to it. Da faddah's a big shot. He's got the Kamehameha suite at the Royal Hawaiian. He'll do right by you if you do this thing for me."

Well, that's how I met Mr. Al Bloomingdale, founder of the Diner's Club. He was the last of the big-time spenders, and he was at Waikiki for the summer with his family. I took care of all their needs on the beach as well as off. I saw to it that his guests, many of whom were international celebrities, were never wanting for anything. Mr. Bloomingdale was one of the most generous, honest men that had ever come to our islands. When the summer was over, he thanked me personally and gave me $2,000.

• • •

David Niven, his wife, and their children visited our shores many times. He was a great kidder and asked me if he could help solicit canoe rides. People on the beach were beside themselves at the sight of David Niven waving a paddle over his head, yelling, "Canoe rides! Canoe rides!" He also rode on all the rides with us.

After one of his trips, he sent a photograph back to us— one he had doctored up on the mainland. It showed him sliding across the face of a 25 foot wave, heading right for the jaws of a huge, man-eating shark. The picture hung above the beach desk at the Outrigger Canoe Club for quite some time.

Chapter 31

The beach boys' job entailed much more than renting boards, giving lessons, and giving canoe rides. There were dinners, picnics, cruises, luaus, and hikes in the mountains. We took the kids ti-leaf sliding when the rains came. All you needed to engage in this old Hawaiian sport was a steep, water-soaked hillside, a freshly picked ti leaf, and rubber bones. After the first few trial slides, the course resembled a toboggan chute, and then the fun would begin. All you had to do was look straight down the hill, place the ti leaf under your *okole*, take off, and pray. Never once on the long rides back to Waikiki, after a day of this, could I remember a conversation that touched on anything but the hair-raising descriptions of each and every ti leaf ride.

• • •

It was an overcast morning and the Moana Coffee Shop was bursting with hotel guests wondering what to do to justify this day's vacation time. I saw her sitting alone by the window, staring wistfully out to sea. She had been on the beach the previous day and rented a backrest from me.

She was a pretty woman, about 35, and tastefully dressed. I bid her good morning and asked if she'd mind if I joined her for coffee. Her response was warm and gracious, as befitting a lady of true substance. I sat down and asked the usual questions. "How long have you been in Honolulu, and how long do you plan to stay?" She told me that this was really just an extended two-day stopover, that she was on her way to Japan to attend her sister's wedding. We commented on the weather and exchanged bits and pieces of our backgrounds.

Her husband was a movie producer. I had seen his name on the screen many times. I suggested that, in view of the weather, this might be a fine day to take a ride up to Nuuanu Pali. She was hesitant at first—more concerned, I sensed, about taking me away from the beach than any impropriety. I told her that it would be my pleasure since I hadn't been on that side of the Island for a long time.

"Well, if that's the case," she said, "I'd love to go. Give me 15 minutes and you've got a date. I've never been up to the Pali."

The trade winds howled and blew with such ferocity that we hooked our arms around each other's waists to maintain our balance. I told her the story of Kamehameha, how he'd pushed an opposing army over the cliffs, and about some guy who had tried to commit suicide by jumping off, and the winds blew him back to his take-off point. We drove down the other side and stopped at a little store just outside Kaneohe. She laughed when I bought some boiled peanuts. I picked up a *paké* banana, peeled it back, and offered her a bite.

"Delicious," she said, and we bought a bunch.

The two-lane road was overgrown on both sides with the lush vegetation of the tropics. The rain came down in buckets—as it so often does on the windward side of the island—and the windshield began to fog up. She wiped it clean with her handkerchief. We drove past the tour buses parked in front of the Crouching Lion, and the name of the little town of Ka'a'awa twisted off her tongue a hundred times before she got the pronunciation right. Clouds parted, and the white sands and azure blue sea of Kahana Bay hung like a picture framed before our eyes. The wind caught a boy's fishing net and spread it flat before it floated down across the water.

"What is this place?" she said.

"Laie," I replied.

"That must mean never-never land," she said.

"That sounds right by me," and I smiled.

The small, tin figure of Karnehameha pointed to the road leading to Waimea Falls. We parked the car at the end of the lane and hiked up the narrow trail. Huge clouds closed like a curtain drawn across a backdrop of blue, and the rain came down, soaking us to the skin. We found shelter in a grove of guava trees, and I delighted in the expression on her face when she caught her first sight of the falls. It had been raining steadily in the mountains and the water cascaded over the cliffs, exploding on impact, creating a fine mist that hung above the rocks and foliage that surrounded the pool. I took her by the hand and led her up to the water's edge.

"Come, let's go for a swim," I said.

"But I don't have a bathing suit," she answered.

I looked at her dress clinging tightly to her body, so wet, so revealing.

"We can swim in the nude," I said.

"No, no, I just can't do that."

"Are you embarrassed? You needn't be. Look, take off your dress. You can go in your underpants and your bra."

"Will anyone come?" she asked.

"Nobody comes up here this time of day."

"Are you quite sure?" she questioned.

"Of course I'm sure. Eh, a few of the local kids come around from time to time to dive off the high cliffs, but if they're not here by now, they're not comin'."

The rain stopped, and the sun peeked out from behind the clouds. She looked up at me trustingly and began to remove the water-soaked garment that clung to her body so tightly. I knew she was shy and having a difficult time, so I turned my back, telling her to hand me the dress when she got it off and I would rinse it and squeeze it dry. I felt her standing close behind me as I laid the dress across the sun-drenched rock, smoothing out the wrinkles as best I could, and then removed my clothes.

Hand in hand we made our way to a low rock where it was deep enough to dive. We swam around in back of the Falls, our bodies touched, and I pulled her to me. We kissed each other for a long time. I pulled myself up on a narrow ledge that ran beneath the raging water, reached for her hand and brought her up beside me. The noise was deafening, and we stood there, screaming and yelling like children in a magic chamber with the moss-covered ceiling and walls of spray.

I put my hand around her and unfastened her bra. She held on to my arms a moment, as if to say, *I'd better not*, and then I felt her grasp relax, and I slid my hand over her *piko* to the side of her hip. I slipped her pants down around her knees and then to her feet. I remember the look of bewilderment on her face, the sudden hint of fear, dissolving to anguish, and then to love. We made love in that private room of ours and her first orgasm came quickly. She begged me to stop, but would not release her hold. I felt her begin to move and our lovemaking continued. Her orgasm was more intense this time, beckoning me to join her.

I took my *ule* out and dove into the river beneath the Falls. When I came up she was laying up against the rocks, and I motioned her to join me. She covered her ears with her hands and shouted above the roar, "I can't! I can't!" I swam back to the rock, climbed up to where she stood, kissed her cheek, took hold of her hand and gently walked her to the other side of the falls.

We drove back out to the ocean and parked the car on the bluff overlooking Waimea Bay. The sky was ablaze with the setting sun, and we sat on the grass in silence, listening to the sounds of the restless sea.

As the lights of Honolulu came up into view she broke the silence that had enveloped us since the colors of the sunset had cast their spell.

"I have never made love like that before," she said. "It was so romantic and exciting. When you stopped the car to watch the sunset, I knew what we had done was very special."

That night, we had a beautiful dinner together on the beach, went back to the hotel, and made love. She left the next day and I never saw her again.

I received a short note from the mainland some time later.

It simply said, "Thank you for my first romantic experience ever, and a day in paradise I'll always remember. Love,"

Chapter 32

Bobby Krewson looked off down the beach and broke into an adaptation of an old song that was popular way back in the forties: *Five by Five* by Don Raye and Gene DePaul...

> *Five feet tall*
> *And five feet wide*
> *Don't measure no mo from head to toe*
> *Than she do from side to side*

"Hey, Nappy! Here comes your girl again."

For the past two weeks, all the guys had been ribbing me about Angela. She was a hefty Italian girl with a great big smile, and that wasn't all: she must have carried 160 pounds on her 5' 2" frame.

Every day, she would show up about eleven and book a surfing lesson from me. The only thing that changed in her routine was the contents in the huge lunch sacks she brought me: Genoa salami sandwiches loaded with Italian peppers; antipasto with a cold zucchini frittata; open-faced prosciutto and cheese on sourdough bread. It was endless.

One night, Angela invited me for a home-cooked meal and served more food than was humanly possible for a single man to consume. One course followed the next, each ending in a vowel. By the end of the evening, I was so full, it was an effort to get up from the table, yet she matched me bite for bite! Then she rolled up on the beach the next day, carrying another large lunch sack. I looked over at Bobby and groaned, "I don't know how much of this I can take. I feel like I got a big lead weight in my stomach!"

Blackout leaned across the counter. "Bet you five bucks you can't take her tandem."

"For five bucks, I ain't walkin' out from behind this stand!"

Bobby took my defense. "Can't you see the man is suffering from indigestion?" Then he smiled and turned to me. "Twenty dollahs sound mo bettah to you?"

"For $20, I'd stand that girl on my ear."

It was on. Bobby called the others. "Hey, Mud! Bunny! We got a bet goin' heah! Nap's gonna try and get that *wahine* up tandem!"

• • •

"Do you mean it? I'd love to try!" Angela was ecstatic, though she knew nothing of the secret bet back at the surfboard stand. I dragged out the big tandem board and explained every move to her: paddling in unison with me, getting up on her hands and feet, feeling my shoulders come up beneath her as I rose up to a tall standing position, while she sat with her legs around my neck. If things went well, she might try standing on my shoulders.

Out in the water, we waited for the right wave to arrive, going over and over the instructions we practiced on the dry land.

"Here she comes!" I said. "Lie down and paddle!"

The wave picked us up, much like the lift you feel in an elevator, and down we came.

"Raise up!" I said, and her broad, heavy *okole* was in the air. But then, just as I slid beneath her, she sat down—all 160 pounds, right on the back of my head! My face squashed against the deck, the board turned sideways down the wave, caught an edge, and over we went.

When I came to the surface, it felt like my nose was broken.

"Guess I sat down too soon, huh?" she said.

"Yes, I guess you did!"

"Could we try again?"

"We ain't gonna quit like this!"

I knew the beach had a thousand eyes, and so out we paddled again. My face was still smarting when the next wave approached.

"Hey, Angela?" I said, and she turned around, with an anxious, excited look on her face. "This time, please don't sit on my face, huh?"

"Don't worry! I won't do that again—at least not out here!"

I swung the board around and we laid down and paddled. The wave humped up to pretty good size, and down the face we flew. With all the strength I could muster, I got her to my shoulders.

"All right!" she yelled. "We did it!"

This time, we rode gracefully all the way to shore.

• • •

We always had a good supply of flower leis hanging from our stand. Hotel maids brought them to us when the tourists threw them away. They were not only decorative, but they provided us with a good excuse to kiss the pretty girls when we gave them away. When Angela and I walked back up to the stand, I grabbed one and put it around her neck.

"This is for you," I said, kissing her on the cheek. "You earned it!"

The Bobby came up and handed me twenty dollars.

"What's that for?" she asked.

The game was up. "The guys made me a bet I couldn't get you up on my shoulders, and we proved 'em wrong. So tonight, you're gonna be *my* guest for dinner. How does the Embassy sound?"

Chapter 33

Quick tours and one-day stopovers—you could spot 'em every time. They stuck out like sore thumbs. And this time, there was no mistaking this group. They walked down the beach wearing wool suits and ties, Sunday dresses and stockings. Religious people out to see the sights.

I saw one of the gentlemen approach Mud. What a guy to ask for information! Mud had his own way of explaining things that took years of training to decipher. They chatted a moment and then you could hear Mud's voice ring out all over the beach.

"Hey, Blackout! I got 15 people ovah heah want to go on one canoe. But dey got no shoats."

"No worry," Blackout yelled back, "I can run 'em in and out. Take two loads."

"Hey, you gonna try put eight people in one canoe?" Mud blared back.

"Just take off shoes. No worry about it, Mud. Go sign 'em up with Nappy."

"Okay, but don't say I nevah told you."

Mud and Blackout were always bickering back and forth about how to do things. "No big waves today," I said. "If you don't mind a little spray, you'll be all right."

Blackout led his followers down to the water's edge and the waiting canoe.

"Where you people from?" I asked the lone abstainer, a frail, unathletic-looking man in a dark blue suit.

"Butler, Missouri," he proudly replied.

When the tide rolled in, they all backed up, and when the water pulled out, Blackout would load. As he was helping the people aboard, additional members of the group began to assemble on the sand.

"Looks like we have three loads now," I said to the little man.

"Yes, looks that way to me, too."

"Be right back," I said. "Somebody wants to rent a board."

When I looked up, Blackout was shoving off. "Here we go!" the people yelled, scratching at the water uselessly with their paddles.

Jeezus, I thought to myself, *he's overloaded!* In his exuberance to accommodate all these strange, dressed-up people, and making sure their clothes would stay nice and dry, he had miscalculated. Not ten yards from shore, they were hit by a small ripple and swamped. People were sitting up to their necks in four feet of water. *Blub, blub, blub.* I could almost hear that sound from where I was.

A swamp was bad enough when everyone was wearing bathing suits. What would these poor souls do? Where would they go? A change of clothes could be miles away. Would they walk? Ride a bus? Mud was beside himself. He started jumping up and down on the beach, yelling, "Hey, Bobby! Nappy! Look out dere! Look at Blackout! He's sunk! I no can believe it! Blackout, you *lolo*! You got too many people in dere!"

Poor Blackout just sat there. What could he say? It was a sad-looking congregation that waded ashore that day.

Chapter 34

"Hey, Nap! Goin' fishing tonight! Tell Steamboat!"

"Mr. Green, my surfing lesson…he goin' come too!"

"I get two or three more *wahines*!"

"Mr. and Mrs. Greenspan. I know they like to come for dinner, too, huh?"

The sun looked like an orange half dollar hanging on the edge of the horizon. Out in the water, we had almost completed the task of laying our nets. In another hour, we will have purchased plate lunches from Wally Yong's store and set up an all-night camp on the beach next to the Royal.

"Hey, how about another beer over heah?"

"Suck 'em up, bruddah! Last call!"

By nine o'clock, we had lashed the two canoes together and pushed off the beach. The fiery torches on the port and starboard sides of the canoe illuminated the waters as our paddles sent us out around the Halekulani. Using three-pronged spears, we jabbed at the reef fish attracted to the surface from the light of the torches. Soon, the beach boys would in our party would dive into the water and take the fish from the nets before heading back to the beach. Music, songs and laughter filled the air off Waikiki until the wee small hours of the morning.

At the first light of dawn, we were back in the water and taking up our nets.

Chapter 35

*Princess Pupule got plenty papaya, she
Loves to give it away, and all the
Beach boys they say, oh meya, oh meya,
You really otta trya little piece of
The Princess Pupule's papaya*

The surf was breaking big off Waikiki—too dangerous that day for the tourists. Board rentals were closed down. I paddled out to a break we call Castles and spent the next four hours doing what I like to do best: surf good waves. When my arms and shoulders told me it was time to go in, I caught my last wave and milked it until it had spent itself just inside the reef. As I lay on my board resting, hands hanging over the side, I felt still high from the excitement of the last wave.

At low tide, the inside break of canoes become a playground, and a woman swam by my board. She was pretty, with long, black hair and big boobs. I had noticed her on the beach for the past few days with her husband and two children.

"Good morning to you," I said, almost too tired to raise my

head off the board. "Do you want a lift to the beach?"

"No, I need the exercise. But I wouldn't mind resting for a moment."

"Hang on," I said, slipping over the side, showing her the way the surfers cling to their board to escape the sun's rays while waiting for a wave to come.

Her arms stretched across the board so that our heads faced one another while our bodies remained submerged under water. Our legs touched beneath the board and my toe accidentally brushed against her private. I waited to be scolded, but her face told me differently. I put my errant toe back where it was and gently moved it back and forth. Once again, I looked to her face for an answer. She approved—and with pleasure—and I felt her foot touching me.

I clung to the board with one hand and tried frantically to unbutton my shorts and unleash my cramped *ule*. Our weightless bodies began to rise up together under the board. At this point verbal directions were unnecessary, and I slid my *ule* into her. There we were, at eleven o'clock on a Waikiki morning, drifting not more than 50 feet from shore, having intercourse.

A canoe loaded with tourists glided by. Blackout leaned over in my direction and said, "Hey, brah. Howz it?"

I took my *ule* out and she swam back to the beach. Later that day, I saw her again, this time with her husband and two children. They were gathering up their belongings, preparing to leave. I walked over, rolled up a mat for them and said, "Hope you enjoyed the beach today, and I expect to see you people back in Hawaii next year."

She gave me a smile. Her husband said, "Thank you," and they departed.

Chapter 36

During the weekends, I was plagued with teenage girls running around the stand. Haole girls from the Outrigger Canoe Club. Their mothers would drop them off, and they would badger me for free canoe rides and offer themselves as tandem partners. Jeez, they'd be fourteen, fifteen, maybe sixteen years old.

Now, one weekend, a young teenager was lingering around my stand. It was about 4:30 and things had begun to slow down.

"Are you waiting for your mother to pick you up?" I asked.

"No. I had a date, but I think I've been stood up."

"Aw, that's no big thing," I said.

Then, out of curiosity, I asked her how old her boyfriend was.

"Thirty-two."

"Thirty-two?! How old are you?"

"Sixteen.'"

"What're you doing with such an old man?"

"Oh, he takes me up to Diamond Head Crater and we fool

around."

"Are you kiddin' me?" I said, flabbergasted.

"Why should I kid you?"

"Hey, well, just for starters, fool around like that up there, you could get *hapai*."

"Oh, we use rubbers," was her straightforward reply.

"Oh."

Sonovabitch, I though to myself.

There was a period of silence, for I couldn't think of what to say next. She said she had been watching me, and when I sat on the canoe she could see my groin from under my shorts, and that made her excited. I asked her if she wanted me to make love to her, and she told me, in the worst way.

"You know, I have an apartment across the street at the Seashore Hotel. Are you ready for that?" I said.

She gave me a coy smile and said, "Sure, but I've got to call my mom first."

"Your mother?!" I was shocked. "What's she got to do with this?"

"She was going to pick me up. I'll have to tell her I've got another ride home with someone from the Club. She's kinda particular who I ride around with."

"All right," I said. "Tell you what. You take this key here and make your call. I'll get somebody to watch the stand and meet you up there in 15 minutes. Okay?"

"Okay. But don't forget to bring a rubber."

• • •

I knocked on the door to my apartment and there she was. When I slipped in and closed the door, she was all over me. Afterwards, I was afraid that the girl would tell her father, and that I might go to jail. For the next week I lived in fear of something like that happening.

The next weekend, she was on the beach again, and she brought a girlfriend with her. They stood around the stand, all talk and giggles. I watched them swim and enter the Hau Terrace for lunch. About three o'clock, she came back and told me that she and her friend would like to make love to me.

I completely forgot how young and pretty they were and told her right away I was shocked. What more could I say? These two girls were by far the prettiest that I had seen anywhere on Waikiki Beach. One of the girls' fathers was a high mucky muck, and the other was just plain rich.

Chapter 37

There was a jukebox in the Huddle Restaurant. It offered 50 selections. Four of the 50 were Harry Belafonte records.

Now, it wasn't that I made a habit of studying jukebox records. It was just that the girl kept playing the same ones over and over again. Sad calypso love songs as only Belafonte could sing them.

A love-struck girl listening to music is no big deal. But this girl was sitting alone in the corner, a half-drunk coke in front of her, crying like crazy. She was a pretty little thing, maybe 30, short hair. I went over to her table.

"Pardon me," I said, "but it saddens me to see you crying like this. Is there anything I can do?"

"Oh, no. I'll be all right," she said, making a rather futile attempt to compose herself. "I guess I've made a bit of a fool of myself."

As she started to get up from the table, her face turned ashen and she fell against me. I carried her outside and set her on the wall, holding her steady with my hands. Whatever it was that caused her to go faint passed as quickly as it had come on.

"Are you okay?" I asked.

"Yes, thank you. Just give me a moment and I'll be fine."

"You're sure?"

"Quite. I've had malaria and once in a while it creeps up on me. That's all."

"Where're you staying?" I asked.

"Right next door, at the Moana."

"Come on. Let me help you to your room."

We took the bathers' elevator to the top floor. When the door opened, she handed me the key. "Do the honors, will you? I'm still a bit shaky."

I glanced at the room number and led her down the hall.

"Could you come in with me? When these things happen, I get sort of spooked. I'd rather not be alone for a while."

I opened the door and she lay down on the bed. "Oh, that's much better now," she sighed and closed her eyes. A gentle breeze filtered through the curtains. They brushed gently against my shoulders as I stood by the window looking down at the beach below.

"I love men with broad shoulders."

I turned and she was sitting up.

"Well, now, that sounds more like it,'" I said.

"Yeah, I think I'm going to live now." She got up off the bed. "Listen, I'm going to take a quick shower, but don't run off, awright?"

"Want me to wash your back?"

"I think I can manage by myself. But pour yourself a drink if you'd like."

"I don't drink during working hours."

"Working?!" she shouted from the bathroom. "What kind of work do you do?"

The shower started and I heard the curtain pull closed. I moved to the half-open door. "I'm a beach boy next to the Surfrider."

"A real live beach boy?" she said, over the noise of the running water.

"That's right."

"What did you say? I can't hear you. I'm washing my hair.'"

I raised my voice. "I said I'll talk to you later, when you get through with your shower."

I closed the door and went back to the window. She was wearing a terrycloth robe when she came back into the room.

"A real live beach boy. I can't believe it. What's your name?'" she asked.

She walked over to the closet and selected some clothes.

"Napoleon."

"You're kidding. Are you hiding from someone?"

"What do you mean?"

"With a name like that, you got to be hiding your real name," and she disappeared again into the john.

"What's yours?"

I was half-shouting again.

"What's my what?"

"Your name. What's your name?"

"Helga. Helga Jorgenson."

When she came out of the bathroom, she was wearing a skirt and buttoning her blouse. It was obvious she wasn't wearing a bra, and the braless look was a no-no in those days.

"Are you a gin rummy player?" she asked. Every time she

moved, I could see her boobs.

"Yeah, I play a little gin."

"Feel lucky?" she asked.

"Hmm, that's my middle name."

She went to the dresser and pulled out a fresh deck of cards. "Are you a gambler?" she asked.

"All my life," I answered.

She stared at me a brief moment. "How about a dollar a point, four hundred point limit?"

That was pretty steep for starters, I thought. *The malaria must have gotten to her brain.*

"Well, I'm game if you are," I said. My friend Cluny, part-time beach boy and full-time card shark, had taught me to cheat at gin and fool a Las Vegas dealer. She didn't worry me in the least.

She removed the cellophane wrapper from the cards and picked up a pad and pencil, and we sat down on the bed. As she began to shuffle the cards, her tits kept staring me in the face.

"Hey, wait a minute," I said. "How do you expect me to concentrate on my cards with your boobs peeking out at me?"

"Sorry about that," she said, and she began to button her blouse. "I'm not trying to seduce you, if that's what you're thinking."

"That's what I was beginning to think," I said. What arrogance. I reached over and felt her breast.

"Uh uh. None of that stuff now. We're here to play cards, remember?"

I stood up and my shorts were bulging. She stared down at me. "Are you always like this?"

I moved up next to her, let her look long and hard, and laid right down on top of her.

"Stop that this minute!" she grunted beneath me. "Get off right now or I'll scream for the manager. I mean it, damn you! I'll—"

I slid my hand up under her dress. She was not wearing panties and her cunt was as wet as Akaka Falls.

"What's all this play action?" I said, and before she could utter another word, my *uli* was in her.

"God, you're too much," she said, her eyes staring up into mine when our love-making had ended. "I hope you don't play gin like you screw!"

During the course of our gin game she told me a fantastic tale about her father having founded a major oil company. She said that she had personally donated over six million dollars to the Albert Schweitzer Foundation in Africa. It was while she was down there working for the good doctor that she contracted malaria, the stuff that was still giving her fits. The talk was big. Maybe she really could afford a dollar a point. I was on my way to taking her for the whole four hundred when the phone rang.

"No, I'm sorry. You can't come up just now. I'm very busy. Never mind what I'm doing, I can't see you right now. You'll just have to call me later. See you soon, huh, Ernie? Okay. Good-bye."

"Ernie!" I exclaimed. "That wasn't Ernie Leashman, was it?"

"Yes, do you know him?"

Did I know him! Huh, he was the hotel manager. "What did he want? Does he know I'm up here?"

"No. He's been trying to get in my pants ever since I got here."

Now, there were the guys that were trying to give the

beachboys a bad name. Here we weren't allowed access to the hotel above the first floor. And the game went on.

"I can't understand this," she said. "I've never been blitzed like this before."

She said she would have to cash a check and would pay me the $400 in the morning. How many times had I heard that before! But I felt sorry for her. She was sick, probably down to her last airline ticket home.

"No big thing. I'll be around the beach."

About six o'clock she came looking for me. We talked a moment and she asked, "What are you doing for dinner?"

I looked at her. "I'm going to have dinner with you," I said.

When I went up to her room and picked her up, she handed me $50.

"Take this," she said, "I invited myself to dinner."

Terrific!

We went down to Fisherman's Wharf and over coffee she handed me four crisp one hundred dollar bills.

"I always pay my debts," she said.

"Hey, no...really, I can't take this. You paid for dinner. You're here on a two-week vacation and if you give me $400, you're going to go home busted."

"I can afford it. I told you, I'm a very rich woman. Besides, I'm not going home from here. I'm going to spend Christmas in France, at my villa. If you feel sorry for me, you're mistaken. Now take this. It's nothing. Believe me!"

Okay. I was almost waiting for someone to come up and take her away.

"Tell you what. I'll take you to a show, my treat. What do you say?"

"Lead on," she said.

The Delta Rhythm Boys were playing at Lau Yee Chai. During the middle of one of the songs she leaned over to me and whispered, "How would you like $10,000?"

"I'd like it," I whispered back. "What for?"

"To buy new things for your business."

"Sounds great."

She squeezed my hand, looked pleased with herself, and the Delta Rhythm Boys sang on.

"Can we go see some hula dancers now?"

The show was over, and I knew this chick was bound and determined to get her $400 back out of me by way of entertainment. After the $10,000 line, I had put her right up on top of my list of all-time con artists. What the hell. I never drop $400 on one girl in a night, ever. I'd still have plenty left over.

She clapped so hard for the hula dancers, I thought her hands would break. We were at the Niu Malu Hotel and she asked if I knew any of the girls, and could I introduce her. I did, but why should I put this line of BS on my friends? It was more than even I could bear up under.

A couple of days later, she was on the beach again, this time holding two airline tickets to Maui in her hand. Now, I was still married at this time, and this would take some doing, but if she wanted to play, what the hell. I was game.

Aboard the plane, halfway to Maui, she started the routine again. She told me she'd been crying that day in the Huddle because Harry Belafonte was an old love of hers and every time she heard his music, it brought back memories that might have been. *Shit*, I thought to myself. *I'd heard 'em all now!*

"You know any other movie stars?" I asked. I was leading her on now.

"Kirk Douglas always stays in my villa when he's on location in France."

I fastened my seat belt a little tighter, and was glad when we landed. *She could be a mad bomber!*

• • •

Hana, Maui had one street. There was a hotel, two churches—one Catholic and one Missionary—one theater, and the Hasegawa General Store. Hilo Hattie made a hit record about this store. Her line was something like, "There lau lau, pipikaula, everything from pins to papayas."

Helga registered at the hotel and I went up the hill to see my friend, Equa Hanchett, who ran the Hana ranch. When I came back to the room, I noticed the two single beds. "Hey, this'll never do," I said, and pushed them together.

"Good thinking," Helga replied. "I like a man who plans ahead."

We changed into our swimming suits and went out to the beach and took a long walk. The sands were deserted, the water an inviting mixture of aquamarine colors. Helga and I made love in the sea and again in the lush green bushes that edged the shore.

When we got back to the hotel, we cleaned up and had dinner. The waitresses doubled as hula dancers, and I knew the girl who took our order and introduced her to Helga. By the time Helga got through dialoguing her, we had front row seats reserved for the show. The girl came to the table after her number and we had drinks together, just the three of us.

When she excused herself to go get changed, Helga asked if I could stay with Equa for the night. She wasn't feeling well. Now there was a fish story I was going to catch her at.

• • •

It was dark walking up to Equa's place, but I only went half way. I doubled back and went directly to the room. I peeked in the window, and there she was with the hula dancer in the room. I tapped at the half open window, and they turned around like kids caught with their hands in the cookie jar.

"Hey, you two!" I said. "Can I watch?"

Everything she could grab on to she threw out the window at me. This time, I did go back to Equa's house. As I was leaving in the morning to go back to the hotel, Equa told me he would like to take us horseback riding that afternoon—that is, of course, if she was still speaking to me.

When I entered the room, she apologized for her actions the previous night, but still thought that was a pretty sneaky trick I had pulled on her. I looked over at the two beds still pushed together, and both had been slept in. I said I understood and we became friends again.

Equa was on the phone when we walked into the stables.

"Uh, huh. Yes, I understand. Yes, I'll tell them." He looked up at us as he hung up the phone. "That was the hotel manager," he said. "I've got some bad news. It seems when the maid went in to clean your room this morning, the beds had been pushed together and both had been slept in. Being a good Catholic, she reported this to the manager. Hotel rules are strict about unmarried people staying together, so they've asked me to tell you that you must find other accommodations."

Equa looked up at me and at Helga, her face flushed with embarrassment.

"'No big thing," I said. "We were only planning to stay one night, anyway."

We rode down the coastline, looking over cliffs to beaches below. Equa opened a gate that had a trail leading down to the sea. The beach was rocky. We tethered the horses and walked out towards the ocean. A tiny stream cut through the sand, embedded with millions of tiny pebbles.

"Look back," Equa said.

There was a huge, 500 foot watercress waterfall pouring over the side of the cliff. We walked up to the base. Equa picked some of the watercress and led us back to the horses. He opened a can of Vienna sausage, took out a loaf of bread and a jar of mayonnaise, and we ate the most delicious sandwiches, all while Helga told us all about her ranch in Ireland. Equa was taking it all in, hook, line and sinker.

• • •

Back in Honolulu, Helga made a reservation at the airport on a midnight flight to L.A. She thought as long as we were going to be business partners, we would have a lot to discuss. *I'd gone along with this phony routine this far*, I thought. *One more dinner couldn't make any difference.*

When I went to pick her up that night, she seemed strangely cold. Over dinner she said she was terribly upset over the fact that I had lied to her, and decided it was not a good idea to give me the $10,000 for our business venture.

"I lied to you?" I said.

"Yes, you did. You told me you were not married and lived

alone in the country. I found out differently and I couldn't possibly go into business with someone who makes up things like this."

After all the crap I'd been subjected to, she was a fine one to talk, but I held my tongue and said I understood how she could feel that way. And that was the last I ever saw of poor, crazy Helga.

• • •

A short time later, Kirk Douglas came to Waikiki to film *In Harm's Way*. Rabbit used to take care of his wife and kids, and one day introduced us. I had nothing to lose, so I said, "I believe we have a mutual friend."

"Oh?" He was taken aback. "Who's that?"

"Helga Jorganson," I said, regretting it as soon as it came out.

"Oh, yah! Helga! Great gal. I always stay in her villa when I'm in France. How's she doing? Poor kid, I don't think she's ever going to get over Harry Belafonte!"

Chapter 38

The honeymoon is over the first time the question "What does your husband do?" is asked. To avoid having to answer, "He's a beachboy," most *haole* women are quick to insist that their new mates quit the beach, immediately. The very thing that attracted her in the first place had become demeaning!

I can only liken such beachboys to a ski instructor, plucked from the mountains and plopped on the beach. His face and neck are burned brown by the sun, but the rest of his body is a pale milky white. He looks and feels strange. Completely out of his element. But Kate was not your everyday *haole* woman. She was different. Picture a big, strapping, blue-eyed, suntanned blonde wearing a two-piece Lynns custom-made bathing suit with an Outrigger emblem sewn on the pants. She could be seen paddling a canoe with a team of Island girls in preparation for a big upcoming race. She could swim and surf and dive and cook. She was nature's child—free of frustration and worldly cares. That was Kate, and she was my wife.

Kate was raised on Oahu. Her father was a well-respected

doctor and it came about quite naturally that she should attend and graduate from Punahou School. We met the year before I left the Island to go searching for my share of fame and fortune that ended with the fruitless search for uranium. Never once were her letters discouraging, and I returned home to compassion and understanding. "I told you so" was not in her vocabulary.

She was proud of my occupation. To be able to make a living in the fresh outdoors, to bring fun and happiness into peoples' lives, was a beautiful thing to Kate. In marriage, as in courtship, we were not only lovers, but the best of friends.

When Kate became pregnant, we mutually decided on natural childbirth for our baby. Mother Nature had been good to us, so it followed that we should continue to respect her ways and reproduce in her prescribed manner. Our people had lived for centuries in her care and her care alone.

My grandfather always told me childbirth was no big thing. If it was so bad and so difficult, where the hell did the human race come from? He had delivered all of his own children and looked upon it as a husband's rightful role in the scheme of the life-giving process. I had been taught, as all my people had, that at birth the woman's breathing must coincide to the movements of our planet and solar system. All living things expand and contract, and the most important thing is to be in tune with the elements. The baby will feel this oneness with all things and enter painlessly into the realm of the living. When the head appears, you must then make ready to lend your hands and soul to the child's deliverance.

We made an appointment with the head of obstetrics at the Kapiolani Hospital and told him of our plans. The doctor sat silently in his chair, nodding his head and shooting skeptical glances first at me and then at Kate.

"You present a noble case, young man," he said to me, "but unfortunately this dream of yours is not based on reality. We have two lives to consider here: that of your wife, and that of your child. It's our job to see to it they are not placed in jeopardy. We have strict rules that prohibit husbands in the delivery room, and they were made for good reason. I've seen too many well-meaning prospective fathers just like yourself pass out at the first sight of blood."

Queens Hospital spared us the long rhetoric. The doctor was tired and brief. "I would suggest to you, Mr. Napoleon, that you stick to your surfboards and leave the delivery of babies to us. You just see to it that he heeds this advice, young lady. Believe me, we'll all be better off!"

Ewa Hospital was privately owned by the plantation. It resembled a rambling one-story country school, built out of wood, always freshly painted and spotlessly clean. The head of obstetrics, a Doctor Anderson from Texas, said yes, he would permit this. Test cases in England were showing that under proper supervision, natural childbirth with the father in attendance could be quite beneficial to mother and child alike.

• • •

When Kate felt that the time was almost at hand, we bought some time at a drive-in movie close to Ewa Beach. When the contractions started, we left for the hospital, and our labors began. After the seemingly endless registration formalities were over, a small Filipino nurse escorted us to the labor room. I helped Kate out of her clothes and into a sacklike hospital gown which tied at the neck and flared open down the back. She lay on the bed and held my hand.

"All set?" I said, "How do you feel?"

"Like I'm about to take off on the biggest wave of my life!"

Dr. Anderson appeared and handed me a hat, mask and gown. He checked Kate's pulse, timed her contractions, called for the nurses, and my wife was wheeled into the delivery room.

"Now, just lay down and try to relax," Dr. Anderson said, as they placed her on the table. "Let's put both your feet in the stirrups here."

"I'd feel better if one leg was free," she said.

"Is that all right with you, Mr. Napoleon?" he asked.

"However she's most comfortable," I replied. "That's the important thing."

At this point, the three Filipino nurses began talking amongst themselves. I looked at the doctor and then turned to the nurses.

"I'm afraid I'm going to have to ask you to be quiet," I said, "It's important to me and my wife. There must be no irritating sounds."

"Well put, doctor," the real doctor said to me. "Shall we proceed?"

It is a belief of the Hawaiians that the birth of a child is like one big sexual orgasm. Prior to and just after the emergence of the infant, the orgasm begins and is so great that it brings the woman's body back to its natural state, now relieved of this living being inside her.

Kate still had one foot in the stirrup and was pushing hard when the water bag broke. I didn't know what to expect. Would the baby just gush forward in the same explosive manner? My father's explicit words on the subject took over, as well as a word of reassurance from the doctor, that I was doing fine. We looked at each other, Kate and I, breathing in unison. Suddenly, a security enveloped us such as we had never before known, and our baby worked its way into my hands.

When the beginning of life appears before your eyes, you know firsthand the meaning of the 'miraculous'. It was a little girl, as yet almost lifeless. I placed her gently on Kate's chest, and Kate, her face drenched in sweat, looked down and said, "Breathe, baby, breathe." Our child began to cry. The doctor showed me how to clamp two sides of the umbilical cord and cut it in the center. He then proceeded to remove the afterbirth.

I would not permit the nurses to remove the baby to the nursery, explaining that the child had been surrounded by its mother's energy for nine months, and these energies should not be interfered with. The moment the baby leaves these energies, the baby begins to die.

Dr. Anderson interceded here, expounding on the dangers of the mother's RH negative blood factor. The child could need an immediate blood transfusion.

"There will be no transfusion," I said. "If a transfusion is necessary, I would rather let the baby die, for it will never be healthy and strong. But this will not be, for the baby is whole, complete, and has a beautiful skin tone."

Jeezus! What was I doing? That's a life and death decision I've just made! But there was no other choice. My decision was founded deep inside me. It's our way.

The doctor was insistent, so he took a sample of blood

from the heel of our baby and a nurse left immediately for the laboratory. The next four hours were agonizing. They seemed endless. Finally, word came back that our child was healthy. I left the room and burst into tears of joy and happiness. We had done it! Kate and I, together.

The baby was asleep by her mother's side when the nurse appeared to take the child for the first of its scheduled feedings. I told the nurse to leave, for this is one of the first things that modern civilization does to a human being. It puts the baby on a schedule of when to eat and when to sleep. It's not to benefit the child; it's done so the parent can tolerate the child. Even before this, at the moment of the child's entry into the world, the infant is picked up by its heels and life, supposedly, is slapped into it. This does two things: it introduces the child into the planet with an act of hostility; and it instills a fear of falling—a fear that can last a lifetime.

I can't deny that it makes me sad that we were unable to make a lasting thing of our marriage, but times and people change. Oddly enough, Kate, a *haole*, was more able to follow the paths of simplicity than I was.

Chapter 39

"Ladies and Gentlemen, the Orchid Room of the Waikiki Tavern proudly presents: Mr. Lenny Bruce!"

We took a party of girls from the hotel to see Lenny perform. He'd been hanging around the beach during the daytime, making quite a hit with all the beach boys. His wife, Honey Harlow, was doing a strip act in the Orchid Room. Lenny was at his worst that night, which was his best. He was dirty and he was insulting and, in Hawaii, a lot of guys aren't receptive to that kind of kidding. I was anxious all night, anticipating some guy charging up the stairs onto the stage and grabbing Lenny by the throat. He was such a little guy, I could see myself in the center of a pretty good beef. Fortunately, nothing happened.

The next day, Bobby and I were walking down Kalakaua Avenue.

"Hey! Nappy! Bobby!" Lenny was leaning over the sixth floor balcony of the Waikiki Biltmore Hotel. He raised both hands over his head like a high priest.

"What you see now is the before!" He turned around and disappeared through the curtains of the hotel room. In an instant, he burst back out onto the balcony again and he was stark naked.

"This is the after!" And he was gone again, and this time he appeared with a partner, a wild-looking girl as naked as he was. He raised her arm with his. "And this, my friends, is the hereafter!"

Whether Honey was in there or not, I don't know. She was another story herself. Honey Harlow, Lenny's wife, would turn tricks between shows in the Orchid Room. What a pair. What a relationship. Was it love? Was it hate? Did I really know the difference? Did they? Did they care?

Chapter 40

"Too hot today to be standin' round like dis," Bobby said, sharing a small piece of shade with me. "Tourist come out heah, he gonna get it two ways: sun will fry his brains and the sand gonna burn up his feet. So, either way, we lose. Dis one da kine no dollah days."

Bobby was right. It was just too damn hot for the beach. We weren't renting a thing.

"How 'bout you and me gettin' something cold to drink? Go down and see Chick Daniels, huh?" I suggested.

"Das da bes idea we've had all day," he answered. "I going drink one whole Par-T-Pak."

It was cooler down by the water's edge. It took our minds off the weather, and as we walked down toward the Royal, Bobby asked me, "You know the *wahine* you were with the other night? She reminds me of da kine lady I picture in Michener's book. Da part he wrote about da guy, Florsheim. How you make out with her?"

"She screwed the eyes out of me. But all the time I had this feelin' she was just puttin' on."

"Wahts' dis 'puttin' on'?" Bobby asked. "You mean all the time she was fakin' it? How could she do dat?"

"I've found—and this is just my own experience talkin' now— that there are two kinds of women. One has feelings and the other has no feelings. And that's the name of that song."

"I think I hear what you're sayin'. Dis interests me. Like da kine prostitute, huh?"

"Exactly," I replied. "A prostitute can tolerate the feeling of being a prostitute. That's why she has no feelings. A woman who has feelings cannot tolerate the feeling of being a prostitute, and that's why she has feelin's. Like my dad used to say, 'If you have to pay for it, it's no bloody good'!"

Chapter 41

Donny Stroud was a beach boy who worked for me. He was the only *haole* beach boy, born and raised in Hawaii. He went to Kaimuki High School. He was a great big, strapping, good-looking guy—a terrific athlete and waterman. His mother was Anne McCormick, one of Jackie Coogan's wives. Donny was a good man to have on the beach. He had all the skills, could play the bongos, sing, and his good looks were really his best asset. If he had a shortcoming, it was his inability to hustle business.

Hawaiian Eye, the television show, was being filmed in Honolulu. A director spotted Donny and used him to double all the stunts for Troy Donahue. I watched him work a couple of times and said to him, "Hey, pal, you're missing the boat. What you gotta do is get in the movies. You're much better looking than that guy Donahue. Why don't you go to the mainland, find yourself some actress—some chick that really knows her way around, that's been there, and could use a guy like you to squire her around to all the places. Pop a few fucks into her and you're going to see your way home, bra. You gonna be home free."

Before long, Donny met Shelley Winters, and—*voom!*—he was on his way.

• • •

People began to gravitate to our stand from the big hotels. Akana and his Hale Au Au began to feel the pinch. Old-timers from the Outrigger resented our encroachment into what they felt was their private domain, never stopping to think that tourist traffic was growing, and the growing demand was more than they could handle, anyway. Hired thugs began showing up at my stand, pulling boards off the racks, and keeping them out in the water all day. A huge man who worked for Earl Akana started hustling business away from my stand.

Fist fights erupted. Guys were waiting for me behind bushes. I started training for survival. At night, I would go home and punch my heavy bag so I wouldn't get a lickin' the next day.

The hotel saw my operation as an open revolt against authority. It was important to them to keep the beach boys in line, under their thumb. Their master plans dictated total control over Waikiki. In 1848, there were approximately 350,000 Hawaiians. Now, our number had dwindled to less than 40,000, all because of this kind of 'authority'. The hotel people got together, contacted Earl Akana and the Outrigger, and a meeting was held at the Moana Hotel. There were representatives from the Governor's Office, the State Attorney General's Office, the Hotel Association, Duke Kahanamoku, the captain of the life guards, and the military people. They formed what became known as the Water Safety Committee. This authoritarian body of men was organized for the sole purpose of getting me off the beach. With the power of a *hui* behind them, they could get State legislators to curtail the activity of freelance beach boys and enact laws to keep us off the beach permanently.

The Committee's purported purpose was to protect the tourists by making the beach boy a certified life guard/bellhop/junior policeman with a sign on his chest—a meaningless badge of merit intended to keep him by means of this title feeling secure, while at the same time a subservient employee of the Establishment. A typical corporate power play. And all of this because one beach boy had the audacity to strike out for himself and make an independent buck off his own rightful heritage. They enacted their rules and regulations, they doled out their titles, all directed at me. Conform, join, or they would see to it that me and my kind were forced off their beach forever. *Huh! Their beach!*

I was subpoenaed into court 14 times in one year on trumped-up charges like interfering with the free flow of traffic on the beach, operating on hotel property, state property, city property. It cost me over $10,000 in attorneys fees in one year alone to keep fighting. As fast as these charges hit the courts, they were thrown out. Nobody really knew just where the proper jurisdiction lay. Where was the high water mark? Still, the pressure and harassment continued. I was beside myself.

I'd been to school. I was no dummy. I knew my way around the block. But in court, I resorted to the old Hawaiian line of defense: "Hey, I don't know dis kind of stuff. Hey, I don't understand you too good!"

"Mr. Napoleon, you do understand right from wrong, don't you?"

"Hey, hey, yeah, brah, I understand somebody hit me, I goin' to hit 'em back. I go store, I buy 5¢ candy, I got pay 5¢."

The only way to be effective was to act dumb, and that I did. The more they talked to me, the less I pretended to understand, and I showed up day after day, day after day, incurring their wrath. But I never backed down.

Chapter 42

The day started fast and picked up speed. I was hungry and harassed. I glanced at my watch. It was almost one o'clock. I called one of the boys to take over for me while I got something to eat.

The Huddle Restaurant was jammed and I waited by the door until there was a vacant seat at the counter. A greasy plate coated with a residue of egg yolk, ketchup and jam, and topped with a cigarette butt, sat before me. The waitress had a pencil stuck in her hair. She picked up the cup and silverware and plopped them on the plate.

"What's the special today?" I asked.

"Spaghetti," she snapped back, removing the appetite killers.

Before I could utter a word she had gone to the kitchen. I watched her take two more orders from people who had come in after I did. It seemed everybody was getting waited on but me. When she finally came back and stood in front of me with her pad and pencil, I talked fast.

"I'd like your special," I said.

"You mean the spaghetti."

"With a smile," I shot back.

Plates of food piled up on the kitchen counter. People were eating and leaving, and still no spaghetti. When she came by I said, "Hey, how about my spaghetti? I gotta get back to work!"

"Listen," she said to me, "You're not the only one in this restaurant, you know. Just because you're a beach boy doesn't mean you're entitled to special privileges."

"Special privileges? I'm not asking for special privileges. Just bring me my spaghetti."

About five minutes later, my order turned up on the kitchen counter and sat there.

"Hey! I think my spaghetti's ready," I said to her.

She gave me a dirty look, picked up the plate, and banged it down on the counter in front of me. Red sauce spilled all over my clean shirt. I looked up at her.

"What the hell are you doing? Look what you've done to my shirt! You know, I feel like stuffin' this down your throat!"

She put her hands defiantly on her hips and snapped, "You just try it!"

I jumped up like a cat, grabbing her by the hair and bending her over the counter. I shoved spaghetti up her nose, in her hair, her ears, all over her face, and before I knew it, her boyfriend, the cook from behind the counter, was on me, swinging like a windmill. I grabbed his shirt with my left hand, pulled him across plates and dishes, and planted a right on the side of his head. He lay motionless on the restaurant floor.

Lau came rushing up to me. "Hey! You can't do that!" and hustled me out the door. By the time the attorneys got through with me, I had a $1500 lunch tab. It had become only too clear that I had reached my breaking point.

Chapter 43

Every Tuesday, a Water Safety Committee meeting was held at the Surfrider Hotel. Things had reached a point whereby I thought I'd better go and make one last big effort on my behalf for those loyal guys that were working for me. I was well prepared and requested floor time. As I was about to speak, Howard Donnelly, the manager of the Surfrider and President of the Water Safety Committee, stood up in a rage.

"You have no business voicing your opinion! I forbid this man to speak," he pointed his finger at me and shouted. "You have no right to be here! What you are doing is illegal—an open, flagrant trespass on hotel property! You should be sitting in jail right this moment!"

I exploded. All my good intentions blew sky-high. "Don't you ever point your finger at me, man! You are nothin'! Nothin' but an employee. I am an employer. You don't even know what that is! Why, I hire and fire punks like you. You tellin' me I don't belong on this beach? Well, let me tell you something. My people been livin' off the sea in Hawaii for as long as I can remember. As long as my grandfather and his father can remember. The ocean's been our way of life! If this beach here, Waikiki, is to become a country club, then it is we, not you, but we, the Hawaiians, who are the charter members!"

And with that I stormed out of the meeting.

My first impulse was to run—to run away from this place this time. I'd had trouble stuffed down me until I was choking on it. So I ran. I ran down the beach to my beach service and told Bobby I had to go away for a while, to take over everything until I got back.

"Where you going?" he asked.

"To talk to my relatives," was my answer.

I caught an airplane and flew to the Island of Kauai. I made my way to the town of Hanalei. I stopped at the Ching Yong Store and bought some supplies, picked up the Kalaulau Trail, and followed it into the Pali wilderness. The Na Pali Coast is Hawaii as it was five hundred, a thousand years ago, and that's just where I wanted to be.

I set up a small camp for myself on Honopu Beach, stripped off all my clothes, and plunged into the sea. The ocean encompassed me like the security of my mother's womb. I once again felt safe. I lived off fruit from the mountains and fish from the sea. I was as at home as if I had never lived anywhere else. For five days, I stayed at this place. I felt the presence of my ancestors and the gods the white men had made taboo for me. The legends that had been handed down from generation to generation came back, and somewhere in this mixture of old and new, the key to my salvation lay hidden.

I sifted through the old class systems of Hawaii, when the people were told what to do by the ruling class known as the Ali'i. It was like a parent-child relationship; the same relationship had been put into play by the missionaries. The hotels were aware of this. Why, some of the *haoles* who started this takeover in 1827 had offspring who are still running things today! They have capitalized on this monarch-subject system and have carried it through to the beach concessions. The beach boys, with one or two exceptions, have responded instinctively.

Everything that had mattered to the Hawaiians died with the last monarch, Queen Liliuokalani, in 1893. Our natural way of life, chants, hulas, the sea, the fishing, died with her.

I thought of my sexual escapades and the beach boys' sexual escapades with white women. What was it that possessed a beach boy to make one conquest after another, week in and week out, without let-up, and then turn right around and reject a woman totally, leaving her in many instances heartbroken?

I came to the conclusion that it was done out of hate. Hate for the white man. It is his only means of reprisal for all that he has lost. He becomes obsessed with the idea of making a conquest over these white girls who come to the Islands, and as soon as he seduces them, they become his slaves.

Then comes the kill: total and complete rejection. And why do these women allow this thing to happen? They, too, are getting even. Maybe with a father, a husband, or who knows? But she is rebelling against society the moment she embraces a dark man, and it is an exciting thing for her. The beach boy picks up on this instinctively, and he preys on her weakness like a hunter. Sometimes he baits his trap with rejection and brings her down with acceptance, all in one motion, which is just what her father did when he would spank her and, after the punishment had been dealt, would comfort her.

She is caught in the middle. It is not love, it is not hate, but confusion. But with all of this, the beach boy does leave her with something. These women find a pleasure and excitement they have never fathomed in all their years. Feelings, long dead, would be reawakened, and they are not lonely, if only for a moment.

My last night alone on the Na Pali Coast was one of those perfect Hawaiian nights. I felt more together and at peace with myself than I had for a long, long time. A million stars shone down and I thought of a girl somewhere on the mainland, and the song she carried home in her heart. It took on a new meaning for me. I wonder if she still sings it?

> Some folks say that love is like a cigarette
> With all its sparkling flame aglow.
> My love for you is a sad refrain
> More than you'll ever know.
> Remember? Only the ashes remain
> My love for you was in vain
> And now this sad refrain is my only song.
> How could you treat me so mean
> To end my beautiful dream
> Of happiness supreme that I knew so well?
> And now the flame of love is gone
> And all because of you.
> Tell me, dear, are you satisfied
> That you and I are through?
> I keep trying in vain to start
> The flame once again
> But only ashes remain of
> The love we knew.

I looked out of the window of the Aloha Airline plane at the shoreline of Honolulu. *Jeezus*, I thought to myself. *The place has grown bigger in just five days!* The Na Pali Coast was buried in the past and perhaps I'd dig it up again sometime. And perhaps I wouldn't. The world keeps on turning and new people coming and, as always, in Waikiki, the beach boy is in the thick of things.

There seemed to be more traffic on the way in from the airport, or maybe I'd never noticed. Kalakaua Avenue was teeming with people. I headed back to the beach to check it all out. To see what I'd missed. To see what was new.

Chapter 44

There was a big party out in Kahala. Rich people from the mainland. A few beach boys were invited to add a little local color to the atmosphere. One of the ladies, the daughter of a movie magnate, who married the owner of a chain of expensive department stores, screwed three of the beach boys in the back yard. Her husband found out and left for the mainland. She stayed on, rented a house in the country, and lived with a beach boy for two more weeks.

• • •

Mr. Shampoo, Gene Shacove, the hair stylist from Beverly Hills who had made a fortune shaping women's heads, would don a floppy hat, set up a stool in the water, and cut our hair for free, dipping a comb and scissors from the local dimestore in the salt water.

• • •

Her husband was in the throes of setting up a new arm

of a giant octopus-like insurance company that had its head in Chicago and tentacles all over the United States and Canada. She used to come down to the beach while he was conducting business. She approached me one day and asked if I would teach her how to surf, that she had to accomplish one thing to justify her trip to the Islands. She learned fast and we became good friends. She would take me to breakfast, lunch, always picked up the tab, and I responded by seeing that she had everything she wanted on the beach: umbrellas, backrests, mats, stuff like that.

I never saw her husband and asked her about this. He was putting in 14 hour days, she said, and this mad schedule was likely to go on for a couple of months, maybe more. She rented one of my boards on a permanent basis, and every day she sat by my stand. When I took out a surfing lesson, she was always nearby, listening for pointers and watching techniques.

She was a neat lady and kinda took a shine to Blackout—not in a big way, but I could see she was attracted to him. He was one of the best-looking guys on the beach.

Her husband finally accomplished his mission and they were making plans to leave. Bobby Krewson told me an unbelievable thing. This lady had offered to give her Cadillac to Blackout. It was brand new. It couldn't have had more than a thousand miles on it. Blackout, out of fear, had refused it. He'd had more than his share of dealings with irate husbands. Anyway, she came down to the beach that afternoon and told me that she was leaving and that she had a present for me. I asked her about this thing with Blackout and she told me it was true.

Kidding, I said, "Hey, Margaret, you just try giving me that Cadillac."

"You want it?" She pulled a pink slip out of her purse, took out a pen and was ready to sign it over to me, right on the spot! I couldn't believe it!

"Hey, look," I said, "I, I can't do that!"

She looked at me and handed me an envelope, saying, "Then take this. It's for you. Aloha."

She kissed me on the cheek and took off. I opened it and it was a check from her trust account for $5,000 endorsed to me. Well, I'd never seen that much money in my life, and Bobby and I ran down Kalakaua Avenue, raced into the bank, and I deposited it into my account. I waited 24 hours, withdrew every dime, five grand, all cash, took it home and buried twenty-five hundred dollars under the house and gave the other twenty-five hundred to Bobby.

Now, four or five months later, her husband flew back to Honolulu. He came down to the beach, walked right up to me and introduced himself. He was fat and chubby and very much older than Margaret. Drawing me aside, out of earshot from anyone, he said, "Napoleon, I just found out my wife gave you $5,000, and I want it all back."

"Hey, no way, pal. That money's long gone—spent, lost, whatever."

"Listen, I know a few people in this town," he said, "and you'd better come up with that money."

"Aw, blow it out your ass. It's too late already."

He stormed off and pretty soon a plain-clothes cop appeared and questioned me about extortion and all that kind of stuff and I resorted to pidgin defense. "Hey, I don't know from dis guy. What you talkin' about, brah?"

And that was the last I ever heard about it—for six months

anyway. And then Margaret showed up on the beach again.

"Hey, Margaret, what are you doing here?"

"My husband was transferred. We're going to be living here now."

"Terrific!" I told her. "I've missed you."

She took right up where she left off and started coming down to the beach every day. We had coffee together one morning, and she seemed pensive. I asked her what was on her mind. Was there anything bothering her? Could I be of help in any way?

She opened her purse and laid a hotel key on the table. "Yes, yes, you can be of help. I've waited a long time to say this. I want to make love to you. There! There, it's out, I feel, I've said it!"

"Out of the clear blue sky you want to make love to me?"

"Let me tell you something," she said. "For six months I sat on this beach fighting this thing. Sometimes it would get so bad I'd have to go in the water and play with myself."

"What?!"

"Now, are you going to meet me up in this room or not?"

I stared right in her face. Let me tell you, it was a pretty good looking face, and I said, "Okay, Margaret. I'll meet you in ten minutes."

I grabbed the key off the table and went to the Reef Hotel. The moment she entered the room she flew at me. She screamed and scratched and moaned and shook. She had orgasm after orgasm, and by the time I had gotten back to the beach, I felt as though I had been through a war.

After this, every time Margaret went out in the water, I looked at her and thought, *Oh, my god, there she goes again*. I told

Bobby, "Hey, brah, I bet we gonna get some more money."

"How you know dis?" he said.

"I'm just getting the feeling, man. I just gettin' the feeling."

Sure enough, a week or so later, there was another envelope and another check, this time for $1,500. Her husband came down to the beach some time later.

"Listen, you. You're not getting another dime off my wife. I'm leaving Honolulu and I'm taking Margaret with me."

Chapter 45

His face was known to millions—one of the biggest TV and radio personalities in the world. He was also the cheapest son of a gun that ever lived. Why, he'd milk a beach boy for all he was worth and then leave without even tipping him. I escorted his daughter and her girlfriend to a big bash out on Diamond Head. The yard was strung with Chinese lanterns and a full orchestra played for dancing.

These were two of the prettiest young girls at the party. Let's call them Sue and Jane. During the course of the evening, I remembered I had the host's swim fins in the back of my car, and knew that if I didn't get them now, something might happen to them. While I was rummaging through the trunk, Sue tapped me on the back.

Startled, I raised up, ready for anything. Anything but her and what followed next.

"I always wanted to kiss a real Hawaiian," she said. "Would you kiss me while there's no one around?"

It was a first for me, too, the first time I'd ever kissed a girl with swim fins in my hand. One kiss led to another and another and another.

"Hey, you better fix your lips and go back inside or we're both gonna be in trouble."

"I didn't bring any lipstick out with me. I'll have to sneak back into the house."

And just like that I watched her run away, like a high school cheerleader.

Sue started to pout when I asked Jane to dance, so at the end of the number I escorted my partner to the table and asked my kissy-faced friend for the next dance. We changed partners back and forth all night. As the party drew to a close, the host asked if I would mind seeing the girls back to the Royal.

"Be happy to," I said.

The girls got their things, we said our good-byes, and left. I stopped the car by the Diamond Head Light House and told the girls about watching the submarine races, an old Hawaiian excuse Island kids use to park and neck. I leaned over and kissed Sue on the cheek.

"Don't want to break a tradition," I said.

"Hey, how about me?" asked Jane.

So, I leaned over farther and kissed her, too. As I bent back toward the steering wheel, Sue kissed me again, on the lips this time, and I went back the other way to even up the score. Pretty soon, I'm going back and forth from one to the other like a pendulum.

On one of my swings I put my hand on Sue's boob. Jane picked up on this and said, "No fair! You didn't do that to me!"

So I did, and back and forth we went again. Now I'm starting to get turned on.

"Don't you think it's my turn?" I said.

"What do you mean?"

"Well, if I'm going to touch you, how about you touchin' me?"

"Oh, God," Jane laughed. "This is terrible."

And I felt Sue's hand squeeze my *ule*. More laughter and then Jane grabbed me. This was fast becoming the neatest fun I'd ever had. I was a little kid again.

"Can I touch yours?" I said.

"Only on top, not bare!" Sue brazenly replied, so I put my hand down between her dress and legs. Jane lifted up off the seat, offering herself, and I felt hers, too.

"Why don't you take mine out and touch it?" I said.

They looked at each other and screamed like two girls in the front row at an Elvis Presley concert. They thought that maybe this was going too far, and I knew they were right. Fun's fun, and no point in wrecking a good time.

We arrived back at the hotel still giggling about submarine races and I took them upstairs. Sue, who had really started the whole thing, was in a room by herself, and Jane was staying with her sister and brother. No one felt sleepy and all of us daringly wicked. So we decided to go into Sue's room just to talk. I hesitated a moment at the door and Sue gave me a little push.

"What's the matter? You chicken of us?"

I reeled backward in an exaggerated fall and landed on the bed. The two girls jumped on me like playful kittens and we wrestled and grabbed and tickled. A button popped on Sue's blouse so she got up and took it off, standing there in her bra.

"Hey, Jane, how about you?" I said.

"And what about you?" she challenged.

"Me?"

"Yeah," Sue piped up.

Jane turned the lights out and added, "Let's all take everything off."

Three shadows peeled off clothing in unison while kisses, hugs, feels and rubs turned into a wild, love-making melee.

The next morning the two girls were sitting on the beach at the far corner of the Royal Hawaiian, hiding behind their dark sunglasses.

"Good morning," I sang out, waving as I walked by on my way to the stand. Sue got up and came running down the beach after me.

"Aren't you even going to come have coffee with us after you embarrassed us so last night?"

"Embarrassed you? Why, I was so embarrassed when I saw you two sitting there, I didn't know what to do!"

"Were you really? Aw, that's neat!"

Over coffee Jane spoke up. "Golly, we've never done anything like that before, ever! You're never going to tell, are you?"

"Uh, uh, not unless we can do it again tonight." And they squealed and screamed with self-conscious delight.

Chapter 46

Somewhere deep in the ocean, off the coast of Chile, the earth had a convulsion that registered over seven points on the Richter scale. Mother Nature did, in one quick moment, what the hotels, with all their laws and manpower, were unable to do: she took away my surfboards and wiped me off the beach.

• • •

I was in the country at a party when the music on the radio was interrupted with a tsunami warning. A tidal wave had just hit Christmas Island and was headed for Oahu and all west-facing beaches. I jumped into the car and raced for Waikiki, and got there just in time to see all my boards and the canoe washing out to sea. My life's blood was draining away.

I jumped into the water and swam like a madman in insane directions. Searchlights surrounded me, police and firemen shouting over bullhorns and loudspeakers. I remember flailing around in circles and seeing every hotel room lit up, and the silhouettes of gawkers at every window and balcony. The water was boiling and suddenly the surge receded and I found myself standing in wet sand, fish jumping and slapping at my side. I'd managed to grab one board, then another. I had three boards in tow when the maelstrom was over.

The next day, Earl Akana and many of the old-timers had smiles on their faces. Huh! Napoleon was wiped out!

"We knew we'd get you, one way or another!"

But I was more determined than ever to wipe those smiles away. A brief encounter from the past flashed in my mind.

I was having coffee in the Huddle Restaurant when this *haole* guy started expounding on the ill treatment he had received in one of the hotels.

He said, "Hawaii would be better off if they'd burn the damn things to the ground!"

In my present state of mind, this kind of talk was music to my ears; after all, the hotels had been trying to burn me.

I realized, of course, that you don't talk rebellion within earshot of the enemy camp, so I spoke up.

"Hey, pal, you're a white man. You come around here making big noises like that, you're going to get your ass kicked!"

"I can take care of myself," he shot back.

And with that, he took me off guard, because this guy didn't look like he could get off the counter stool without help. He must have been, of, jeez, 65. He was physically sloppy and his dress matched equally. So I said, "Well, listen, your beef ain't nothing to me except I happen to agree with you, and if some guy comes up and calls you, I don't feel too much like beefin' today."

He looked me up and down, pulled hard on his cigar and

exhaled through crooked, tobacco-stained teeth. "Hey, you're all right, you know that, kid? I like ya. In fact, I could use a guy like you."

"Me? What're you talkin' about?"

He told me he was a friend of Chuck Uehara, and Chuck was the guy I had leased our canoe from, and that he'd been nosing around Waikiki looking for investment opportunities. That our chance meeting in the Huddle that morning was not really by chance, that he had already talked to Chuck about me and checked me out and knew more of my predicament with the Committee, and that his tirade against the hotels was for my benefit. And he wanted to test my reactions. I said that was all quite flattering but I was doing pretty well on my own. I was learning to live with harassment.

"Well, listen, if you should ever change your mind and want to go to war with them bastards over at the hotel—eh, I mean in a big way—look me up."

He gave me a business card, San Francisco address, and the name, number of an attorney he retained in Honolulu. With that he got up, extended a grimy and surprisingly strong hand, breathed a rancid breath in my face, and just as quickly as he had appeared in my life, he was gone.

Later that afternoon, I asked Chuck about this guy.

"Yeah, weird guy, but he's for real. He has enough dough to back up anything he said."

I filed Mr. Barney's card in my wallet and promptly forgot about him. But man, I never forgot about his breath!

• • •

Now, I had three mangled surfboards and enough money

to see me through the next week and a half. Where the hell was that card! I got on an airplane with a dream and a prayer and I went to San Francisco to see Mr. Barney. Chuck was right. He was for real. He had nine kids, lived on the Presidio Terrace in a $300,000 home, and took me to lunch in his brand-new Lincoln Continental.

He listened attentively to my story of the tidal wave and how it had left me, literally, on the beach. And when I was through he took a long, big cigar, lit it, and spoke directly at me through a veil of grey-blue smoke.

"Did you ever dream of becoming a millionaire, Barry?"

"Who hasn't?" I replied.

"Well, let me tell you something. If you listen to me, do exactly as I tell ya, I can see a million dollars apiece clear for the both of us. You see, kid, I'm a guy who does his homework. And I know more about you than maybe you know about yourself. But go on, give me your pitch. But let me forewarn you. I got eyes in the back of my head, and I've already stolen the catcher's signs."

We went back to his office and he went directly to his desk, pulled out a book of checks and wrote out a big one for $5,000.

"This is for starters, Barry. From here on out, we're co-partners. 50–50. You put up the know-how, I put up the dough. Now, you go do whatever it is you have to do, and I'll draw up the necessary papers."

Just as quickly as that I was back in business. But, more importantly, I suddenly felt a security I had never known. I was no longer alone. I had a man behind me. He got me a huge truck-trailer and I drove from San Francisco to Dana Point, California, bought 25 brand-new Hobie surfboards, turned right around to San Francisco, loaded them aboard the ship, and flew back to Honolulu.

I rented a cubicle in the Waikiki Arcade Building next to the old Steiner estate. Copies of the business papers arrived from Mr. Barney, and the Bohemian Surfboard Company was formed. I was off the beach yet on the beach, and no damn hotel could tell me how to run my business, who I should be nice to, who I shouldn't be nice to, when I could take off and go surf, when I could go to the bathroom. I could now independently think for myself without harassment.

Mr. Barney came to Honolulu to survey what I had done with our starter money. He liked the price of our rented cubicle ($65 a month) and told me to take on another. He asked me if I was prepared to sweat it out for a bit, so that the business could test its wings and fly on its own for a while. He put me on a $600 a month draw and, as our bank account grew, so did our business. Within a year's time, we had four surfboard stands up and down Waikiki Beach.

The lease on the entire Beach Center came up for bid. I excitedly got on the phone to San Francisco to Mr. Barney. He said that he did not think this was a good move at the time for we could use the money for a bigger operation he had in mind. Actually, it was an operation I had presented and talked to him about many times, but it now became his idea. I asked him if he would mind if I raised the money on my own. I would gladly put it into the business, but I felt ownership of the Beach Center was an opportunity we should not let slip through our hands.

"You got moxie, kid," was his answer. "I like that. Go ahead."

I flew to the mainland and went to see Mr. Bloomingdale. I told him of my plan and what it would take to win the bid. Mr.

Bloomingdale loaned me the money to buy the Beach Center. Our rental was now kicked up to $3,000 a month and, hell, we made that in a week. New surfboards kept arriving from the mainland so that we could meet our demands. The sport of surfing was mushrooming. Waikiki tourist business was going crazy.

Mr. Barney started coming to Honolulu more and more frequently, rubbing his hands together and chortling with glee. We always had dinner together, and he kept hitting on me to keep him supplied with a little feminine companionship, while at the same time preaching to me the importance of watching my Ps and Qs.

"It's for your own sake, as well as that of the business, Barry," he would say. "You never want to shit where you eat."

Mr. Barney felt it was time to put our new plan into operation. We would buy out Dale Velzy and start mass producing our own surfboards. Surfboards within the reach of the people, pop-outs that everyone could afford. To do this, we dissolved the Bohemian Surfboard Company and threw it into a new parent corporation called Accurate Systems. "The corporation is responsible only to itself," he told me. "Real protection for the both of us. Yeah, you're building an empire for yourself. Don't want to lose that."

I put the first surfboards in Sears, Roebuck & Co. They sold like hotcakes.

I was ridin' high. When celebrities came over to the Islands, they called on me personally—not as a beach boy, but as a friend.

Every bit of money we took in went back to San Francisco, along with the records, purchase orders, and receipts. Even my

$600 check was mailed out of San Francisco. Now, living on $600 had not been easy, but I kept thinking of what was piling up in the Accurate Systems account, and how it was being put to work, 'mainland style'.

I called to ask my partner for a larger draw, not much, a few hundred bucks. I felt this was more than justified by the huge amounts of money our business was bringing in. The knockout came fast, the punch was unseen and lethal.

"Why, it's apparent you have no conception of how high our costs have been running! I've not seen a dime off my investment, in fact, the truth of the matter is we're on the brink of bankruptcy!"

"Bankruptcy!" I shouted. "On the money I've been sending you? Bullshit! That's impossible!"

"It's right here in front of me. I was just going over the figures, and figures, my friend, don't lie."

I hung up the phone. What the hell was going on? What was he trying to pull? I knew exactly how much money went into the manufacture of boards, costs of sales, profit margins. I'd signed the lease on the Arcade, took care of the concession stands. Who did he think he was kidding? My attorney, who was also Mr. Barney's attorney here in Honolulu, hit me with a lot of legal gobbledy-gook designed to keep any layman at bay. That was a waste of a phone call and left me wondering whose side he was on. Maybe I'd caught my partner at the wrong time of the month. I'd just let it go for now and have a serious talk with him in person on his next trip. It came sooner than I had anticipated.

"The accountants have advised me to salvage what I can out of this mess. If we liquidate the whole shebang, sell everything, lock, stock and barrel, I might just be able to come away with what I put into this thing."

I looked at the guy sitting across from me and couldn't believe what I was hearing. He reached into his briefcase and withdrew a bunch of legal papers. When we had incorporated into Accurate Systems, I had literally signed my life away; on paper I wasn't even a factor in our Hawaiian Village operation. He had everything neatly tucked away in his back pocket. Everything I had built, everything I had worked for would soon be gone. One more Hawaiian flushed down the tubes, and it was all there in front of me in black and white.

Chapter 47

Hawaii is a land of contrasts. Nature has endowed her with elements that work together to produce a variety of endless wonder and beauty. White clouds float across deep blue skies. Brightly-colored flowers perfume the air. Burnt orange soil turned on mantels of green grows tropical fruit of every variety. Countless species of fish, every shape and pigment, abound in the sea. Reefs of coral form blue lagoons that wash up on sun-baked sands of white and black. The sun shines when it rains. Ethnic groups, dark and light, burley and slight, have come together, bringing into being a new breed of golden people. They create their own contrasts—social, economic, good and bad.

There is Diamond Head—with luxurious estates fronting back yards of palm-lined beaches—and Kalihi shacks—termite-infested and roofed with weathered tin that snaps and pops in reaction to the sun's hot rays. There is Waikiki, with swanky stores, posh hotels, rich tourists, and expensive restaurants. There is downtown Honolulu and Hotel Street, seedly flophouses over tattoo parlors, Pacific derelicts in dark doorways. Mormon temples, Shinto shrines, polo matches, and cockfights.

Anything is everywhere, and in-between is a standoff. I've seen them all, and I know them well—the winners, the losers, and those in the middle of the pack. But where the hell am I?

I'm on the beach. I have nothing. Yesterday, I owned more surfboards and canoes than maybe anybody in the world. I controlled 90 percent of all the beach concessions in Waikiki. Today, I have one 12-foot tandem board to my name. I'm 35 years old, and I don't even have a car. I look out upon an endless sea for some sign, some answer to my dilemma. None is forthcoming—only the knowledge that the farther I drift away from my shores, the more perilous the journey becomes.

A gentle rain passes overhead. A rainbow bridges the gap from sea to shore, ending at the foot of Diamond Head, and I have my sign.

I moved into a small apartment on Nohonani Street, two blocks from the beach. In the morning, I'd go down to the Halekulani where my surfboard was stored, have a strong cup of coffee, and begin again.

I paddled down in front of the Moana Hotel and started hustling surfing lessons. I had to rent my surfboards. I charged $7 for a lesson and kicked back a dollar and a half to the concessionaire. I averaged $20 to $30 a day, taking solace in the fact that there were worse lots in life than being a beach boy.

On slow afternoons, I went diving with my good friends, Bobby and Freddy. Freddy was fearless, and Bobby laughed at everything. One one day, a giant sea turtle stalked Bobby, opening and closing its powerful jaws. Bobby backed off, laughing, pushing water at the aggressor's face. Freddy saw this and swam straight into the monster. The turtle dove and swam away.

A club of completely outfitted scuba divers from the mainland were talking about the hazards of freediving. One member dropped a spear in deep water, and before they could muster a plan of recovery, Freddy went down 80 feet and plucked it off the bottom. And let me tell you, 80 feet straight down in the ocean with just mask and fins was like two miles.

There were long rides home from the country after dark, Bobby talking all the time, relating funny encounters with the tourists.

"What do you call that fish over there?"
"Yellow fish."
Or,
"What's the difference between a porpoise and a dolphin?"
"Same kind."
Then,
"Man, dis guy comes down to da beach yesterday, wearing so many gold chains around his neck he could win the title. Big! Like da kine toilet chains."

We would stop to eat in little Japanese restaurants downtown that served tok won, saimin and rice. On Kapahulu Avenue, it was Ono's for pipikaula, lau lau, lomi salmon and poi.

I found a girlfriend—a wholesome-looking blond, just 18 years old. She was the daughter of a Brigadier General stationed somewhere in the midwest, and her name was Jan. We were good for each other, Jan and me. We filled a portion of each other's empty spaces.

. . .

Three o'clock in the morning was when it hurt the worst. There is no lonelier time for a troubled spirit. I would awaken to the Barney thing gnawing at my insides, extracting sweat from my body. I felt the walls and ceiling of the tiny apartment, like time, closing in and a bed was no place to be. Sometimes I would walk down to the beach and just wait for the day to begin.

Seven o'clock in the morning: it felt like noon, yet the beach was scarcely awake. The doors to the snack shop opened and I wondered if she would be there again. For three straight mornings, we had shared the counter, drinking coffee, saying nothing. Perhaps she, too, felt like me, almost afraid to violate the sanctuary of the morning after battling the tempests of the night before. But as the sun moved higher in the sky and the beach came alive with people, night ghosts would recede like the tide. Life goes on.

I asked my brother, Nathan, if he knew anything about this woman who had now taken on the qualities of a girl in a bikini and was laying on the sand.

"You can forget about that one right now," he said. "She's awfully rich and she's got way too much class for you. You couldn't touch her with a 10-foot pole."

"Thanks a lot," I said. "Just thought I'd ask."

And with that, I got on my board and paddled off to work.

It was lunchtime when I walked down to the water and back up on the beach. My brother was talking to her. The next morning, the counter at the snack shop was empty, except for me. I kept looking at my watch and waiting, but she never showed up. It was time to go to work, and I felt a small wave of loss sweep over me.

• • •

The big tandem board scraped against the sides of the locker. It felt 10 pounds heavier than the day before. I looked up and saw her spreading a towel on the sand. I shoved the board back in its place and decided to try another tack.

"Hey, Eric! Come over here for a minute, brah!"

Eric was a beach boy of few words, but those that he said were often direct.

"You know that *wahine* sitting over there?"

"Sure."

"Introduce me to her, will ya?"

"Okay."

We walked over to her towel.

"Dis is my friend, Barry."

She nodded. Eric walked away and I sank to my knees in the sand.

"I like that," she said.

"You like what?"

"The way you handled our introduction. Why, most guys would walk right up with a cute remark they've practiced a hundred times and spend the next twenty minutes boring me to death. We've seen each other every other morning for the past three days, and you respected my 'alone' time. I appreciate that."

Barbara was from San Francisco. She told me she had made several trips to the Islands the past few months, decided it was a pretty good place to be, had purchased and just moved into a new house out on Diamond Head. She seemed surprised by my knowledge of San Francisco, the people I knew there, the associations I had made.

"You're not the everyday, run-of-the-mill beach boy. Why are you doing what you're doing?"

"It affords me the time I need to paint."

"You're..." and she delayed a moment "...an artist?"

"An aspiring artist."

"How exciting!"

Barbara was a collector, and when you can afford to be a collector, there's nothing more challenging than to become a patron. I knew I had stumbled upon a common denominator.

She couldn't wait to show off her art works to someone with an appreciative eye. We left the beach and drove off towards Diamond Head.

Royal Circle curved down through Lauhala trees enshrouded with bougainvillea and stopped at the beach. Night-blooming cereus reached for the sea, and palm trees and hibiscus were everywhere.

The old frame house had a steep sloping roof indigenous to the South Seas. The back lawn ran to a sea wall made from black lava rock. Water-soaked coconuts dotted the sands, and waves cracked over the outside reef. Two divers carrying masks, spears, and a sackful of fish passed by a few feet from the car.

"*Howzit?*" one says.

"Fine, bruddah. Just fine."

She had an old-fashioned kitchen, copper pots and cookware hung from the walls. And the living room was just that: every piece of furniture was made for comfort and blending into an overall scheme of beach house decor.

"Now," she said. "You *must* see my pride and joy!"

She led me up a narrow staircase to the master bedroom. A huge, four-post bed—the kind one would expect to find in New England seaport towns like New Bedford or Nantucket—stood high off the floor. A huge painting—an oil of the windswept sea—hung over the bed. She pulled the curtains open and the light streaming in from the window fell across the center of the canvas, like the sun breaking out from the clouds.

I turned to her. She looked so small, standing there in front of the big bay window, her light auburn hair draped neatly down, curling around the collar of a turquoise beach coat, belted tightly around the waist, flaring open to reveal slim but very shapely legs. We stood there for a moment in silence, staring at one another, and I started to unbutton my pants. She never moved. Her eyes never left me. I stood in front of her, completely naked, held out my hands, and drew her next to me. Her arms hung loosely down at her sides as I untied the sash of her beach coat. I took off her top and then slid her bikini bottoms down to the floor. We moved to the bed and made love, never saying a word.

I left her laying on the bed, put on my trunks, walked down the stairs and out the folding glass doors in the living room. The sun was warm, the breeze was fresh. I hopped off the sea wall, made my way across the sand and dove into the sea. She was sitting on the sea wall when I returned to shore. I walked up to her, pulled myself up on the wall, and sat down.

"Why did you do that?" she said.

"Because I've been wanting to fuck you ever since the first day I saw you. If you're upset about it, I'm sorry. It happened, and that's the way it is."

She didn't say anything. She just sat there, staring at me, turning her head slightly from side to side.

"Look, I'll see you around. Okay?"

I pushed off the wall and walked off down the beach. She came running after me.

"Wait. Wait a minute." She caught up to me, put her arm through mine and said,

"Don't go away from me, all right?"

I looked down at her. She forced a smile, saying, "Well, the least you could do is buy a gal some breakfast!"

We drove back to the Halekulani, ordered fresh papaya, Portuguese sausage, and eggs. Over cups of steaming hot coffee, she told me a lot about herself. My brother Nathan was right about one thing: she was a very rich lady.

Chapter 48

The sun was setting over a calm sea. The breeze was barely audible through the palms. Waikiki Beach was quiet once again.

A small group of Hawaiian singers was serenading on the terrace of the Halekulani. The tables were all occupied by happy, suntanned faces. Barbara looked radiant. The flower lei I'd given her covered her tan, slender shoulders—all the wrap any girl needed on a night like this.

A waitress in a bright-colored muumuu came over to the table to take our drink order. I suggested two Mai Tais. No one reproduced the Mai Tais they put together in the Islands. They almost resembled large fruit cups; a fresh pineapple spear would protrude through the ice, a sprig of fresh mint would hang on the rim of the glass, and a cherry would float aimlessly in the translucent, rum-colored liquid. Visitors seemed to delight in having one of these drinks placed before them. Instead, Barbara ordered a Gibson on the rocks.

A couple of honeymooners at the next table requested

Kekali Neiau. I explained to Barbara that this was our Hawaiian wedding song, best sung by a man and a woman in two parts, like reciting vows.

The waitress came by and Barbara nonchalantly ordered another Gibson. I had not even finished eating my pineapple spear.

Once inside the dining room, the waiter asked, "Would you care for cocktails before dinner?"

"I think that might be nice," Barbara answered. "What are you going to have, Barry?"

"Nothing for me this time." I'd already begun to feel a slight glow from my Mai Tai.

"Oh, don't be a poop! Have something!"

"Okay," I said. "Bring me a Mai Tai." I was starving. The least I could do was eat the pineapple.

"And I'll have a Vodka Martini on the rocks. And very, very dry, please." She had two more drinks before dinner arrived.

• • •

It was after ten o'clock when we got back to Royal Place. She invited me in for a nightcap. She told me to make myself comfortable in the living room and then she headed for the kitchen. I heard the crack of an ice tray and she called out, "Any special preference?"

"Just a little wine would be fine," I answered.

She returned with a freshly opened bottle of Mateus on a tray, one wine glass, and a tall Collins glass filled to the brim with ice and what I took to be water. Nobody could put that much Vodka in a glass, plan to drink it, and survive!

By eleven o'clock, she was smashed. I carried her upstairs,

helped her out of her clothes, and put her in bed. She reached out and grabbed my hand.

"Commmere…" The two words slid together. "Take off your clothes, too."

I did, and crawled in bed beside her.

Chapter 49

"And just where were you all night?" Jan said.

I was still wearing my good clothes from the night before.

"Playing poker," I said.

"Uh-huh." She was suspicious. "And since when do you dress up like that to play poker?"

"Eh, it was a high-class game."

"And it lasted all night?"

"Til five o'clock. Then I went for breakfast."

"You sure look rested for someone who's been up all night."

"Wish I felt as good as you say I look. I got a big day today."

When I came in from my surfing lessons that afternoon, there was a telephone message for me at the surfboard stand. No name, just a number. I dialed and Barbara answered the phone. She was bright and cheery.

"I guess we really tied one on last night, didn't we?"

She hardly gave me time to answer. "I've been to the market and I've planned a wonderful dinner for us tonight. Please tell me you can come."

"What time do you want me?"

"Any time you can make it. I thought we'd eat around 7:00."

"I'll see you before then," I said, and hung up the phone.

I asked my brother Allan if I could borrow his car again.

"Put some gas in it," he said, tossing me the keys in the air.

Jan wasn't at the apartment. I showered, changed, and left a note telling her I had another poker game on.

There was still plenty of light left in the day when I knocked on the door, opened it a crack, and yelled, "Hey, anybody home?"

She came flying out of the kitchen, tripped on the rug, and landed, sprawled at my feet. I bent down to help her up.

"Are you hurt?"

"Naw, I'm all right. God damn that rug!"

Her breath reeked of alcohol. I took her over to the couch. She raised her dress above the knees and the swelling had already begun. She rubbed her knee with both hands and holding back a sob, said, "Barry, do be a darling and go make me a drink."

I opened the refrigerator and it was practically empty. Whatever she had planned for dinner was nowhere in evidence.

Before nine o'clock, she had passed out on the couch. I gently carried her upstairs to the bedroom, undressed her, and made her comfortable. Then I went downstairs, watched TV for about an hour, and went back to my apartment.

• • •

Jan was reading a pocketbook novel when I opened the door.

"I thought you were playing poker again?" she said.

"Aw, one of the guys didn't show up," I said, opening the refrigerator door. I was starving. I poured a large glass of milk and grabbed a handful of cookies from the pantry.

"We never have enough legs in our poker game."

I kissed her on the cheek and devoured my cookies and milk. It was good to be home.

• • •

I had no trouble sleeping that night. I arose early the next morning, full of good intentions to make this a prosperous day. I stayed down by the Moana all day long. I had a full schedule, and when my last lesson was over, I was tired and well satisfied with myself.

I saw Barbara standing on the beach when I was still a hundred yards offshore, and I felt like paddling back out to sea.

"I missed you for coffee this morning." She flashed the same forced smile I had seen that first day on the beach at Black Point, and she walked beside me to the surfboard rack.

"Hey, listen, I gotta work for a living."

"I know, I know. I don't mean to be a pest, it's just that I enjoy being with you so much."

I didn't say anything and started to put my board away.

"I was talking to some people today and they told me about this perfectly charming little place up in Manoa called The Waioli Tea Room. I made some reservations. You will go up there for dinner with me, won't you? I'll be good, I promise, please! Let me make up for last night."

"Barbara, let me tell you something. It takes every penny I make just to get by. I don't even have a car. I've been using my brother's and I don't feel like asking him to use it again."

"Then let me rent us a car, and I'll be heartbroken if you don't let me take you to dinner."

"Okay," I said. "What time are your reservations?"

"Eight o'clock. Is that too late?"

"Eight is fine. Why don't you pick me up on Beach Walk and Kalakaua."

• • •

Barbara didn't drink that night or any other night for the next two weeks. Jan was upset by my nightly carousing. I offered one phony excuse after the other, and I could tell she wasn't buying any of it. She kept the misgivings to herself. Our conversations became strained. We were pulling apart, but neither of us had any place to go.

Barbara had to return to San Francisco. When she left, she told me I could use the car as long as I liked, and that she'd already made arrangements for the billing. I got phone calls from the mainland every day. It became a standing joke on the beach. The last time she called, she asked me if I could take a week off and visit her in San Francisco. I'd been planning to go see my mother and father anyway. They were living near Oakland, and I'd just been waiting to collect enough money.

"Sure, I can do that," I said.

"Fabulous! I'll wire you a ticket."

Chapter 50

A thick mantle of white fog hung off the coast of California below. We descended down through a wispy-thin layer of the stuff, and the airport lights stretched out before us. The big plane touched down, I heaved a sigh of relief, and heard the stewardess announce it was 10:00 p.m. Pacific Standard Time.

In the baggage claim area, I looked around through the milling people, but Barbara was nowhere in sight. I spotted my suitcase riding down the conveyor belt and made a grab for it, then backed my way out of the crowd.

"Excuse me. You're Mr. Napoleon?"

She had a heavy German accent, short blond hair, and steely blue eyes. A big woman. She was the kind you used to see playing the part of a womens' prison guard in the old World War II movies about Nazi Germany.

"Yes," I answered. "I'm Barry."

"My name is Ilse, and Barbara has sent me to pick you up. She's not feeling well."

She turned, and I followed her out to the parking lot.

• • •

Pacific Heights, Baker Street. The station wagon climbed the steep grade and turned into the narrow garage bored into the side of the hill. The houses all measured about 50 feet across and rose up three and four stories. The steps leading to the front porch were made from highly polished marble. Two Monterey dwarf pines grew up out of pots at least four feet across that looked like they'd been raised from the same marble and hand formed. A huge door, hewn from solid mahogany, was highly polished, and a solid brass knocker awaited callers like a vibrant drum begging to be pounded. White rugs lay upon solid oak-pegged floors in the entryway, and a crystal chandelier hung over my head from a tall ceiling. I looked up at this glowing monster, sparkling and twinkling, and my eyes fell upon Barbara, standing by the railing on the second floor.

"For Christ's sake! I thought you'd never get here!"

She was drunker than a lord, and I thought to myself, standing there with my bag still in my hand, *What the hell am I doing here?*

I looked around and Ilse was gone.

"Well, don't just stand there like a statue, get your buns up here! Aren't you glad to see me?"

The stairway seemed ten miles high. I wished it was higher. It wasn't. I reached the top. (In a way, I wondered I had reached the bottom.) She threw her arms around me and led me into the bedroom.

"If you could have seen yourself standing down there. You looked like a statue. You did! Just like a friggin' stone statue! Here! Put that silly bag down."

I placed my suitcase down on the floor, next to the wall.

"Now take your coat off. Here, here, let me help you."

She fumbled and pulled at my jacket, dancing around me, and I just stood there, motionless. She threw my jacket on a chair and jumped on the bed.

"Now, come here! I've been waiting two long weeks to see you, and I want you to fuck me. God damn it, fuck me now!"

I stared down at this confused, alcohol-ridden, poor little rich girl. Hell, she was far worse off than I was. All right, I had accepted the ticket, the free ride. If that's what she wanted, I would pay my dues.

• • •

Barbara had passed out cold on the bed. I was sweaty and tired. It had been a long day. All I wanted to do was stand under a nice, hot shower. The bathroom was bigger than my entire apartment. To use it almost seemed a sacrilege. The mirrors, the tiles, the fixtures—all were sparkling clean. There was fresh soap and thick, rich, monogrammed towels. I let the water beat down upon my body for a long time. I filled my mouth, washed my hair, lathered, rinsed and lathered up again. When I stepped out onto the lush pile bath mat and toweled dry, I began to feel human again.

I had no desire to crawl back into that bed. Still, I didn't know where to go. Like a stranger in strange surroundings.

I put on a change of clothes and stepped out into the hall. Ilse was walking down the staircase.

"Hey, hold it!" She stopped still and turned around, her face expressionless. "Is there anything to eat around here?"

"It's very late. I will call downstairs and have the cook make you something."

"Hey, no…it's not that big a thing. I can go out and get something."

"There's not much open at this time of night. I can make you a sandwich."

"You sure that's not too much trouble?"

"It'll be no trouble at all. Why don't you go upstairs to the third floor. There's a solarium up there. I'm sure you will find it quite comfortable."

"Thank you. I will."

As I climbed the stairs and I thought to myself, *That's the spookiest wahine I've ever met in my life*. At this juncture, I felt that nothing in the world could surprise me. I was wrong. The room was a showplace. The walls were made of glass, and the entire city of San Francisco, from the Golden Gate to the Oakland Bay Bridge, lay at my feet. I stood there, absorbing every light, every movement, and time stood still.

A rumbling noise broke into my reverie like a loud fart in church. I turned around to see the wall open. A light went on and some food was sitting there on a tray. A voice came out and said, "Here's your sandwich, Mr. Napoleon. I took the liberty of choosing a German beer for you. If it's not to your liking, just press the button and I will try to accommodate you. Good night."

I didn't know who the hell was talking, and then it registered. It was Ilse. "Good night," I babbled.

I was all alone at the top of the world, and I wanted to come back down. I ate my sandwich and turned on the TV, then turned it off again. I put my empty tray back into the wall and walked downstairs. The lights were off in Barbara's bedroom, though I couldn't remember turning them out. I walked down the hall and opened another door. The light from the hallway streamed in and a little girl was in bed, cuddled next to a big panda doll. I eased the door closed again. I tried another door. A small boy was sleeping.

Where am I? What's going on? She never told me about any of this. I descended another flight of stairs. I was back in the entryway. I walked through the dining room and into the kitchen. Nobody had told me where I was going to sleep, and I was frightened to death to go on searching for fear I'd bump into Ilse. I noticed a phone on the kitchen wall and I called an old girlfriend of mine who had moved to the Bay Area about a year ago. As far as I knew, she wasn't married or living with anyone, but at this point I didn't care. I needed a friend.

"It's good to hear you," she said. "Where are you?"

"I'm in San Francisco."

"You're kidding! Can you come over?"

"Just tell me how to get there," I answered.

The keys to the station wagon were hanging on a ring right next to the phone. I put them in my pocket and walked out the door.

• • •

The last time I saw this girl, they were calling her flight number. She was smothered in leis, tears streaming down her face. I kissed her *aloha* and watched her board the plane.

I considered for a moment how my life had changed drastically in just one year. I wondered what time had done to her.

"Aloha, and welcome to San Francisco!" She threw her

arms around me and kissed me hard on the mouth. Then she stepped back, saying, "Let me look at you."

She was wearing a flowered kimono, her hair was neatly brushed, her face, lips and eyes freshly attended to. But the year had taken its toll. We took right up where we'd left off, though after what I'd just been through, it wasn't easy. Her bed was warm and soft.

• • •

The next morning, traffic was heavy and it was after nine o'clock when I arrived back in Pacific Heights. Ilse came to the door and let me in.

"Where in the hell did you disappear to?" Barbara said, sitting in the kitchen and drinking a cup of coffee.

"Hey, you passed out on me last night. Your maid went to sleep. I didn't know what the hell to do, so I went and got me a hotel room."

"Oh, for Christ's sake! We've got so much room in this place. Shit! You could have slept in the guest room. You could've even lowered yourself and slept with me. We're not exactly strangers, remember?"

She looked frazzled and hung over, and ten years older than she did in Honolulu. I sat down at the coffee table and rubbed my eyes.

"Could I have a cup of coffee, please?"

"The pot's on the stove, cups in the cupboard above. Feel more at home now?"

I got up and poured myself some coffee.

"Barbara, do you remember that day at the Halekulani when I told you about myself? Now, granted, there wasn't much to tell, but still, it wasn't easy for me. Now I think you owe *me* an explanation. I took time off from my job to come over here and see you. Last night was a disaster, and I really don't know what the hell I'm doing here. And I know very little about you!"

She stared into her coffee cup, swirled the inky black liquid around, then looked up and changed into that innocent little girl smile of hers.

"Guess I wasn't too cute, was I?"

I didn't say anything. I could tell she was about to unload.

"It's all here, isn't it? Anything anyone could ever want. The end result of the American Dream."

She got up from the table, cup in hand, and continued her dialogue, pacing back and forth - at times looking directly at me, at others using the windows and walls as prompters.

"Shit, it's more like a goddamned nightmare! I'm an heiress. Don't I look like an heiress, Barry?" She ran her fingers through her tousled hair, her hand was shaking. "Look at me. See what wonders money can bring? My mother and I control the stock of one of this nation's biggest banks. Half of the Board of Directors are scared shitless of me. Anything I want is just a phone call away. I have two live-in maids, a cook, and a handyman. The only thing I have to do for myself is wipe my ass. Oh, I've done wonders with my life. I've fucked up two marriages. I got two kids who are afraid to go to sleep without the lights on and need special tutors to hang on in school. I drink too much and I haven't got the guts to do anything about it. I run away from everything. That's why I bought the house in Honolulu. Nobody knows me there, and I never would've come back if it hadn't been for the kids. The least thing I can do for them is to see that they're not uprooted in the middle of a school year. Maybe by summer the lawyers will have taken care of my divorce settlement, and I can start anew and be me for a change, whoever the hell that is!"

My head was still spinning as I drove across the Oakland Bay Bridge, heading for my parents' house in Alameda. She had told me that she was in love with me—that she felt a peace and inner security she had never known before when she was with me in Honolulu. She wanted me to move in with her until we could both return to Hawaii together. Man, I was in the middle of a heavy, heavy scene.

• • •

It was close to midnight when I left the folks. Mother had prepared a Hawaiian dinner, and the entire evening had been light and gay. It was my intention to keep things that way. Sure, I'd stay with Barbara until it was time to go. If I could help her in any way, I would. If I could make it worth my while in the process, I would do that, too. She could afford it.

We drove down to Carmel and checked into the Del Monte Lodge. Barbara bought me a new set of golf clubs, shoes, shirt, sweater and slacks, and walked the Pebble Beach Course with me. We had dinner at Gallatin's, an old house in Monterey converted into a restaurant. When the waiter asked us if we wanted cocktails, I said no. Barbara stuck her tongue out at me and we laughed.

You could make a career out of going to lunch and dinner in San Francisco. I tasted saltimbocca for the first time at Doros on Montgomery Street. Barbara told me it meant "jump in the mouth"—and she was right! It was a sautéed veal that had a flavor like nothing else of its kind.

At the Lake Merced Country Club, when we requested a starting time, I was made to feel like Lee Trevino. At Kan's on Grant Avenue, it was my turn. I ordered bitter melon soup, Peking duck with plum sauce, and steamed fishes of every variety. Paolo's, Chez Marguerite, front row center at the Curran Theatre—we did it all. Brother, we didn't miss a thing!

"I have a surprise for you today," Barbara said. We hopped on a cable car and headed down Van Ness Street. The sharply dressed salesman in the Lincoln Mercury showroom handed me the keys to a brand-new Continental convertible.

"I hope you like the color, dear. It's a special paint. Don't you just love it?" she said.

"I love it."

I looked at the salesman. He had a phony smile on his face. I thought to myself, *Okay, pal, so we both made out. You got a fat commission and I got a car.*

• • •

Low clouds and fog hovered over San Francisco. A week's vacation had turned into three, and my thoughts were turned toward home. Mother invited me to dinner when I called to tell her I would be leaving soon. Barbara complained of not feeling well, so I went alone. I was just as glad.

When I got back, Barbara was not in her room. Both cars were in the garage. Perhaps she was upstairs in the solarium. I went up to check, but it was dark. There was a crack of light under Ilse's door and I heard voices, so I gently knocked. Barbara came to the door in her bathrobe. She had a funny look on her face.

"What's up? What's happening?"

"Just talking to Ilse about the children."

She whisked by me and went to her bedroom. Before the door closed, I noticed Ilse was in bed. Her back was turned, facing the door; a portion of the covers were pulled back and she was naked.

• • •

Even though I kept all of my clothes in the guest room, I got a funny feeling staying around that house. I felt out of place. The kids and their tutors were always coming in and out; Ilse was like an iceberg; the cook, I'm sure, was feeling put upon by having an extra mouth to feed. The upstairs maid began to get a bit too familiar with curious questions, and when the groceries were delivered, there were always a couple of bottles of booze in the bag. I began to suspect that Barbara was closet drinking, maintaining a constant level of high that I had been too busy—or naive—to ascertain.

I found a photograph of a big, buxom, muscular woman sitting beside a pool in a bathing suit. There was writing in the lower lefthand corner. It said, "To Barbara, All my love, Helga."

When I asked Barbara if she was a Russian shot-putter, she got miffed.

• • •

Barbara had a business luncheon with her mother and some high-ranking members of the bank. I was in the solarium watching television when she returned.

"The old shit really hit the fan today," she said. "Mother's found out you're staying here and is having a cow over it. You should have heard her ranting on and on, like, 'You get that horrid Filipino man out of this house. I won't tolerate that kind of thing going on!'"

"What'd you say to her?" I asked.

"Told her in so many words to fuck off! What I do is none of her goddamned business!"

It was obvious Barbara had been drinking. It was also obvious that it was time for me to go home.

Chapter 51

Jan had moved out. I couldn't blame her. Hell, I would've done the same thing. There were now two suitcases to unpack, filled mostly with clothes ill-suited to a warm climate. I felt like a first-class gigolo.

Lewers Road runs into the Halekulani. The pavement felt hot on my bare feet. Three weeks of wearing shoes had softened them up. I ordered a cup of coffee and looked out at the Pacific. Had it all been a dream? As I was leaving to get my surfboard, the phone rang.

"Hey, Barry, it's for you."

I picked up the phone. "Hello?"

"This is Barbara."

"Barbara! Where the hell are you?" I asked.

By this time, nothing that crazy chick might do could surprise me. She could have followed me all the way over here, for all I knew.

"I'm in San Francisco going crazy without you! I want you to come back."

"I just got here. No way!"

"There's nothing for you there any more, and you know it as well as I do."

I was dumbfounded, at a complete loss as to what to say—except maybe, "Fuck you."

"Give up your apartment, Barry, and move back here with me."

"Listen, you gotta be crazy! What about my car? It's even being shipped back here."

"I cancelled that."

"You what?!"

"Now, don't be mad, it's right here waiting for you."

"Listen, I can't come back there again on some whim—car or no car. You want me to come back there? You send me five thousand dollars. This time I want to be independent. Then, if something comes of this thing, okay. If no, then okay, too. That's all I'm gonna say."

I hung up. Four days later, the money arrived in a plain envelope, no note. Just a big-assed check made out to me for $5,000. I put $4,000 in the bank and ten crisp $100 bills in my pocket. That night, I took all my beachboy friends to dinner and we watched the lights go out in Waikiki. On Saturday afternoon, I got on the big plane. It was like watching an instant replay with myself as the star. Ilse met me at the airport. It was cold and gray.

"Where's Barbara? In the bottle again?"

"Barbara has gone to Oregon."

"Gone to Oregon? I just talked to her not more than six hours ago! She told me she would be here, and—"

"She'll be home tomorrow."

We rode back to Pacific Heights in silence. The hot coffee was beginning to melt the chill when the upstairs maid came into the kitchen. The old gossip had come fishing.

"The coffee smells good," she said. "Mind if I join you?"

"Not at all. Please sit down."

She poured herself a cup and we began to talk.

"You don't get along well with Ilse, do you?" she began.

"I think it's mutual," I replied.

She lowered her voice. "I can't stand her, either. You know, she takes advantage of Barbara."

"Oh? How's that?"

"Barbara paid her boyfriend's fare to come over here from Germany," she said.

"Well, Barbara is a very generous woman."

"But there's more to it than that." The upstairs maid was rolling now and I knew she couldn't stop. "They're making this."

She rubbed her two fingers together.

"Oh, really?" I smiled. "What's that?"

"They make love together."

"Who makes love together? She and her boyfriend? What's wrong with that?"

"I'm talking about Ilse and Barbara."

She went on to tell me that Barbara had really gone to Oregon to see another girlfriend, that her name was Helga, and they had been 'intimate' for a long time. "She keeps her picture in her bedroom."

• • •

I walked up to the top of the steep hill. The wind was blowing a gale. What do I care? This whole thing is nothing more than a passing fancy. I'm here for a fling and to have me a good time. I got a girl on 19th Avenue, I know another girl lives up in Concord. I was still getting letters from a co-ed in Berkeley. Shit, I got money in my pocket and $4,000 in the bank and a brand-new Lincoln Continental. What do I care about dis kine of stuff?

My new shoes had leather soles and heels. I made a start and slid back down the hill like I was on a big wave. I took the station wagon and drove down to the airport to meet Barbara. She waved frantically, pushing her way through the crowd and threw her arms around me.

"It's so good to see you! Mmmmm," she said, as she held me tight. "It seemed like years!"

"Yeah. I got here yesterday and you missed me so much you went to Oregon."

"It was an impossible situation, Barry. Don't be upset."

She put her arm in mine and we walked to the baggage counter.

"This very dear old friend of mine called me. She was frightfully upset. It was a money thing. Oh, not much, really—but the world to her. I just had to go and straighten things out for her. It's all settled now and you're here and I'm here and we have each other. What else matters?"

• • •

The Bayshore Freeway felt like a crowded race course to me. Everybody, it seemed, was always trying to outmaneuver the other guy.

"You seem concerned about something," Barbara said. "Driving makes you nervous?"

"No," I replied, staring at the road.

"Anything wrong?" she asked.

"Just thinking."

"Care to let me in on it?"

When nature calls, you seek release. Once I started, I couldn't stop.

"Isn't it true that the real reason you went to Oregon wasn't for money, but love?"

"That's crazy! What are you talking about?"

"No, it's not crazy. I happen to know it's true."

That was a staggering blow I delivered. She was dazed and reeling. I moved in. "I don't care. It's your business. All I'm askin' is for you to be honest with me."

"I don't know what to say," she stammered.

"Start from the beginning. We've still got a long drive ahead of us. Believe me, I'm a big boy. I won't think any less of you. I'm Hawaiian, remember?"

She waited, gathered her thoughts, and began. "When I was going to school, my girlfriend and I, we were roommates. We used to crawl in bed together. It was nothing, really. We'd kind of hug and make each other feel good. Then, once, I was in this hospital in New York, and I met a nurse. Helga. We became friendly and she invited me to meet her in the city. I couldn't help myself and she made love to me in a way I can't ever forget. When she called and said she was lonely for me, I couldn't resist and went to see her."

She never mentioned Ilse.

• • •

We hadn't been in the house five minutes when out came

the booze.

The road to hell is paved with good intentions. Every morning, Barbara swore off the stuff, and every night, she started in again. I spent my days playing golf, eating long lunches, and shopping with and without Barbara.

I met a couple of guys at the golf course. We used to gamble our way through 18 holes over every course in San Francisco. Late one afternoon, we were having a few beers after the game. The steaks smelled good and we ordered dinner. It was after nine o'clock when I got home. Barbara was usually dead to the world by this time. I went upstairs to her room. It was dark inside. There was a light on in the bathroom. I heard the water pouring out of the faucet and into the tub. A funny feeling came over me and I eased the door open, just a crack. Ilse was giving Barbara a bath. I stepped back, closing the door as carefully as I had opened it, crept out of the bedroom, made my way in the dark upstairs, and lay down on the solarium floor.

Walls have ears and so do floors. I knew when it was time to go back to the bedroom. I wrapped my hand tightly around the doorknob. It opened noiselessly, and I entered. My eyes had grown accustomed to the dark and there was no mistaking what was going on. Blankets and top sheet were pulled back to the foot of the bed. They were both naked. Ilse was bent over Barbara, kissing her on the mouth, one hand stroking expertly over her boobs, and the fingers of her other hand pressed in tightly between her legs.

I stood there watching—a dark, silent, unseen figure. Barbara was cooing and so obviously drunk she didn't know what was going on, and I knew she would draw a total blank in the morning. I stole closer to the bed and put my hand in the crack of Ilse's ass. She was on fire. Startled, she looked up and I was on the bed, my hand rubbing the soft wet hair between her legs. Ilse started to pull away from Barbara, but I forced her hands back to where they were. "Make her come," I whispered, and she put her tongue between Barbara's legs. After Barbara had an orgasm, I unbuckled my belt and unzipped my pants, rolled Ilse toward me, half on her side, and I slipped in her as smooth as jelly.

• • •

Barbara had a monumental hangover the next morning. We sat at the breakfast table, sipping black coffee. She asked about my golf game and where I had had dinner. Before I could answer, Ilse came into the kitchen and poured herself a cup of coffee. At that moment, it became clear that Barbara had known exactly what was going on last night.

"Ilse, get me a pencil and a piece of paper, will you? I've got to make up a menu for Saturday's luncheon. Maybe you can help me. I'm a little foggy this morning."

Ilse and I glanced at each other. Nobody said anything about it, and it was never brought up again. *What a life*, I thought to myself.

• • •

Barbara, I knew, really hated herself for drinking like she did. It was a constant battle with the bottle. She drifted in and out like a jellyfish caught in the tide. When she was off, things were beautiful. When she was on, well, that's another story.

One Sunday, we took the kids to Golden Gate Park. That, afternoon, the 49ers were playing at Kezar Stadium. We had seats right on the 50 yard line. After the game, in spite of the cokes and hot dogs, the children were still hungry, so we drove to Fisherman's Wharf and ate shrimp at the Grotto. It had been a super day.

That night, I helped put the kids to bed and took a shower. When I came into the bedroom, Barbara was standing there with two glasses and a full bottle of champagne.

"Celebration time," she said. "It's not every Sunday those goddamned 49ers win a football game!"

We touched our glasses together. I took a sip and set mine aside. Barbara drained hers and reached for the bottle. I was faster, and held it away from her, saying, "This is the last piece of booze we're having in this house. Otherwise, I'm leaving right now, and you know I mean that."

The bottle and those two glasses never moved from her nightstand, and I never questioned her reasoning behind this. Whatever it was, it seemed to work.

Chapter 52

Sea lions barked from somewhere out in the fog. Gulls lined the shore like grounded aircraft. We walked upon the wet sand, clinging to each other for warmth and security. What courtship, I wondered, was worth its salt, that hasn't known stormy seas? We left that night for Acapulco.

Las Brisas is built into the side of a hill overlooking the bay. Each individual apartment unit has its own private swimming pool. It was good to feel the warm sun on my skin again. We explored the beaches and swam in the sea. Barbara took on a healthy radiance I had never known before.

The back streets of Acapulco reminded me of the poorer sections of Kalihi and Palama. Barbara was uneasy here, but I wanted her to see it. We took a crowded bus to the silver city of Taxco and returned to our hillside hideout with all manner of ornate jewelry.

We held hands on the long plane ride back to San Francisco. A thick stack of mail filled the letter holder on the bedroom desk, a stark reminder that no matter how far away one goes, or how long the stay, the world is laying in wait for you. One important-looking envelope was from a law firm with five names. Barbara's estranged husband had gotten word of my being in the house and was demanding custody of the two children unless I left the premises immediately. I moved into a small motel room and we lived like thieves in the night.

There's no honor among thieves, legal or illegal. Every night, I would sneak back down to the house and leave with the first light of dawn. We put the big home up for sale and moved into a smaller place on Green Street—the big advantage being that it had an elevator that ran down to the garage. We had an electronically-controlled garage door installed. It was activated by a control panel in the car. Life became a game of hide-and-seek. To be seen was to lose. I would climb over the motel back fence, set up clandestine meetings with Barbara, and hide in the back seat of the car. To any curious onlooker, it appeared that Barbara always entered and left the house alone. But detectives are not just curious onlookers. Our every movement was recorded and reported. The court ordered the children to be placed in the custody of their father.

I felt terrible about what had happened. Not only had I grown quite fond of those kids, I knew how much their loss meant to Barbara and what it might do to her. We became constant companions in a world of facades. Two people going through the motions but never entering the arena. We put the furniture in storage, the cars in a boat and went back home to Honolulu.

The house on Royal Place had been sold. We stayed in a hotel until we found a place on Kulumanu Street, right off Black Point. Doris Duke had built a waterfront mansion here, which sat upon a small bluff like a monument to affluency. She brought in the engineers, built a breakwater, and created her own little harbor. A small access channel cut through the reef, but as long as I could remember, I'd never seen a boat moored here. A narrow ledge led from the beach and fronted a 50-foot sea wall that guarded the palatial home from intruders. Local kids would dive from the rocky ledge and bask in the sun. Fishermen planted themselves on the rock jetty to cast high and far out into the ocean. The placid waters of the harbor afford a dandy place to spearfish.

Life was for living. It was easy and sweet. Our days were full and the time flew by. Barbara had the furniture shipped from San Francisco to our new home just off the fairway of the Waialae Kahala Golf Course. In the eyes of my family, I had arrived.

• • •

My older brother, Nathan, came up to the house in a state of panic. His partner was selling the beach service out from under him. They had two concessions, ideally located at Fort DeRussy and the Halekulani Hotel. After what had happened to me, I was itching to reestablish myself on the beach. Nathan's predicament afforded just the toehold I was looking for.

"What will it take to buy him out?" I asked.

"Twenty-five thousand," he replied.

Now, for 51 percent, that was a lot of bread, but hell, I was rolling in dough and Nathan knew it.

"Nathan, you got yourself a new partner," I said.

• • •

Shortly after Barbara's divorce was finalized, we decided to get married. We flew to Reno and became respectable citizens once again. My parents were thrilled with Barbara, particularly my mother. I had made it bigger than any *haole* she ever knew. We stopped and visited the kids in Tiberon, located across the bay from San Francisco. It was obvious Barbara's ex was having some problems. She called her attorney and told him of her misgivings about the children's welfare. The attorney gloated over the fact that I was now 'gainfully employed' and, quite possibly, he said, the courts would now look favorably over our change in circumstance.

Barbara said Mrs. Hahn was cold on the telephone when she called to inform her of our marriage. She did manage a "I hope you will be very happy over what you've done," before she hung up, however. We sang the old Ethel Waters song *Miss Otis Regrets* on the way to the airport.

A few months later, Barbara's ex stubbed his toe, so to speak. Lawyers served their summons, the court looked askance, and the children were sent to Hawaii to live with us. Our creditability continued to grow. Even my new mother-in-law broke her long silence by sending Barbara and I an invitation to a family reunion in San Francisco.

We were whisked away from the airport in a chauffeur-driven limousine to a big house that sat even higher up on the hill than Barbara's old house had. I wondered if there was any social significance in this, like "the higher you get, the higher you get." Looks of curiosity mixed with cautious optimism greeted us on our arrival. No doubt about it: here, I was a different breed of cat.

Mrs. Hahn hugged her daughter and offered me her hand.

"Barry, it's so good to see you."

Christ, I'd lived down the hill from her for almost a year, and had never seen her before this. She was dressed like a queen, with hair and clothes and diamonds all reflecting elegant good taste. None of this helped. She was the ugliest-looking woman I'd ever seen in my life.

Barbara introduced me to her two uncles, their wives, and children. They were dressed to the teeth and called me Mr. Napoleon.

"You two must be exhausted after your long flight," Mrs. Hahn said, anticipating a lull in the conversation after the first how-do-you-dos. "You'll find everything waiting for you upstairs in the guest room, Barbara. Dinner will be served at 7:00. Of course you will join us for cocktails in the living room."

My first thought was, somebody stole our suitcases. However, the butler had discreetly taken them upstairs to our room. We had already been unpacked and our clothes neatly put away. An old-fashioned bathtub stood on brass bear claws. I asked Barbara where the shower was.

"You're looking at it," she replied.

I didn't want to get in for fear of leaving a ring around the tub. Maids were everywhere. Matisse, Van Gogh, Renoir, Frederick Remington - originals all - embossed the living room walls. We sat on antique furniture, uncomfortably beautiful, and discussed the weather, politics, hippies, and the decline of practically everybody.

"Dinner is served, Mrs. Hahn." It was the French maid. Her announcement was practiced and slipped right into the dead air time in the conversation. The dining room was set up to resemble a state dinner for visiting dignitaries. A banquet-sized table was set with fine Porthault linen. Hand-pounded English sterling graced the Crown Derby china. Tiny silver spoons were buried in dainty salt and pepper dishes. There were wine glasses and white goblets and antique crystal. A vase of fresh spring flowers was set between two fine sterling five-arm candelabrum. Everything to make a guy feel right at home.

The maid was dressed in a black uniform with a starched, white pinafore and cap to match. They glided in and out between our chairs serving cold watercress soup, Belgian endive salad, poached salmon with hollandaise, and whole tiny potatoes with waists. There was a sumptuous peach melba dessert followed, of course, by a demitasse of coffee and Limoges finger bowls. Brandy and cigars followed in the library.

Chapter 53

"We will have to tailor the coat."

The little man, with a mouthful of pins, sweated profusely and talked while he chalked. "His shoulders are too wide for his waist. The pants we got no problem. I can take a pair off a 39 regular."

I was being outfitted with formal evening clothes so I could go to the San Francisco Opera House, get out of a limo, walk on a red carpet, and squirm through three hours of some Wagnerian classic. As I stood looking at myself in the three-way mirror, I thought, *Boy, could Freddy Noa or Bobby Krewson have fun with this one!*

After our shopping spree, we picked up Mrs. Hahn, had dinner, and took in a show. As we were walking to the car, two ladies of the evening approached, high heels, black mesh stockings, faces made up like kewpie dolls. One of the ladies had on a bright red satin dress and a fox stole with the face still on it. The thing was really sad looking, both the face and the fur. I looked at her, and she looked at me.

"Nappy!" she screamed, and threw her arms around me. I lifted her off the ground and spun her around.

"Legs! Howzit?"

Crazy Legs Griffin used to be an exotic dancer at the Blue Lei and Club Hubba Hubba in Honolulu. She was the original 44D girl. These girls used to hang out on the beach during the day. Beachboys were always being queried by male customers as to the availability of female companions. Dinner companions, you understand. We knew them all. The girls were good to us and we were good to them.

Crazy Legs was an especially good friend of mine. One day, I was standing alone in the board room of Hale Au Au when Legs came by, her 44Ds bursting out of her top.

"You know, Legs, one of these times I'm going to tear that top right off of you and see those things up close and first hand."

"No need to get rough," she said, and she untied her top and wiggled those monsters in front of me. Hmmm! That was Crazy Legs, and here she was, her dancing days over, a victim of time.

Legs backed off quickly after she realized how she had let her emotions get away and the unprofessional mistake she had made. But I let her know we were friends, and you can't buy those.

Mrs. Hahn was speechless all the way home. And Barbara could hardly keep a straight face for the laughter that was bottled up inside her.

Chapter 54

The Hahn ranch spread over 5,000 acres in the foothills of Santa Rosa. The main house was designed and decorated to resemble an early California ranch. Paintings by Mexican artists, leather furniture, wagon wheels, spurs and saddles were everywhere. It even had its own vintner set up in an ivy-covered rock building out in back.

Mrs. Hahn called for a jeep and, as I had expressed a desire to go riding, she had a horse saddled for me. We covered every nook and cranny of that property, riding through herds of prize cattle, and stopping to rest by trout streams and reservoirs.

The guest cottage was a home in itself, three bedrooms, three full baths. Cowboy boots of all sizes were placed in built-in racks, hats from sixes to eights hung on wooden pegs, and drawers full of Levis and shirts—a stock to make any Western haberdasher proud—filled hand-carved bureaus.

Barbara's mother went back to the city and left us to our own devices. Her departure was cordial, if not a bit cold. She seemed satisfied that she had discharged a debt to her daughter.

The ranch foreman was a big, tough, burly guy. He took me fishing and hunting. I even helped to round up some cattle. This was my kind of place. I really had the fever, and Barbara had it, too. Some women take to horses like swimmers take to the water. Barbara was one of these gals. She spent hours at the stables.

"If I could transport this place to Hawaii, I would do it in an instant," she said.

I told her I knew of places about an hour from our home where we could have all the horses we wanted.

"Then it's settled," she said. "I was almost ready to leave you for this horse here, but you talked yourself into another chance. You ready to go back?"

"I just left," I said.

Chapter 55

Haleiwa is on Oahu's North Shore. We refer to this area as 'the country.' We bought a piece of property right on the beach. We talked and drew our own plans and started building our house. When it was finished, we had 6,000 square feet under the roof. A small waterfall ran through the living room. There were separate servants' quarters, a tennis court, and even an Olympic-size swimming pool. (No matter that the best swimming in the world was right out the front door.) We installed a big electric gate, and a chain link fence kept the dogs inside.

We leased some acreage across the street. The stables went up and we went horse hunting. Barbara wanted to breed and raise pure Arabians—a tall order in Hawaii. We attended every horse show and auction that came along, and that's how I met my friend Tuna Sampaio. He sold us our first horse.

Tuna lived way up at the top of Pupukea behind Waimea Falls. He was the ranch foreman for Charley Peach. Peach owned all of Waimea Falls down to the bridge on the highway.

It branched out above the Falls and spread out all over the Waimea Valley. Wild goats and pigs roamed the lush green hills. Old Hawaiian *heiaus* stood sacred and protected. Macadamia nuts, sweet Hawaiian oranges, and melon-sized guavas grew in profusion. Water ran everywhere, and herds of cattle and spirited horses had the run of the range.

Tuna cared no whit for anything but his horses, the land, and a few trusted friends. He was content to live in a saddle, indifferent to life's modern luxuries and conveniences; just the kind of man Mr. Peach wanted to oversee the running of his ranch.

Tuna was one tough *paniolo*, and Charley Peach was no slouch, either. He was a heavy-set, fair-skinned man. He was raised in Hawaii, and after a few drinks can talk local with the best of them. He matched Conrad Hilton dollar for dollar, and together they built the Hilton Hawaiian Hotel. Peach sold his interest and bought the Mark Hopkins in San Francisco. Mrs. Peach was a great horse enthusiast. She had show horses, jumpers, polo ponies, and ranch horses. She could ride them all. Tuna respected this and took every pain to serve her well.

Tuna Sampaio introduced Barbara and I to these people and their ranch, and that was the beginning of a very wonderful relationship. The gates were always open to us, Barbara learning more and more about her horses, especially from Mrs. Peach. And Charley and Tuna exposed me to experiences far beyond my wildest dreams. The four of us would often ride the Waimea Valley together, looking at rare birds, wild orchids, and building a friendship that was to be one of the high points in my country living experience.

The Peaches had a huge riding arena that was roofed

over and contained 20 horse stalls. Tuna and I used to take the jumping fences down, saddle up the polo ponies, and ride the late afternoons away.

I bought my own string of ponies and all the tack, boots, hats, pants, and saddles. We joined the Mokuleia Polo Club. The season started and, from then on, it was polo every Sunday. The season was four months long, and Barbara and I became permanent fixtures.

Chapter 56

Tuna raised fighting cocks. He'd pad their feet like boxing gloves and square the birds off against one another to fight. If one chicken turned its back on the other, he'd take a stick and knock its head off.

"Man, what the hell did you do that for?"

"What do I need a damned chicken that's scared to fight?"

On Thursday afternoons after work, Tuna would load his fighting cocks into the truck. Cowboys would jump into the back and we'd all head down the hill for Waialua.

Waialua is an old town. It was built for the workers who still labored in the pineapple and sugar cane fields of Dole and Del Monte. It's flatland, for the most part, and lies between the rolling hills and the sea.

A dirt, rut-scarred road led to a cluster of old wooden plantation houses, almost hidden from view by the overgrowth of tropic vegetation. *Haole* faces were a rarity out there. Dust flies and roosters crowed as the truck bounced around a bend and into a cul-de-sac. Cars were jammed into every available nook. The atmosphere was reminiscent of a traveling gypsy carnival, come to play.

Off to the left, small wooden stands were set up under some trees. Hand-painted signs offered fresh vegetables, fish, meat sticks, chicken, and pastries. Washtubs half-filled with ice and water were packed full of soda water and beer. Children played games, darting in and out of the trees as grandmothers sat in groups, hiding from the hot sun beneath the protective branches.

A long shed-like affair, roofed and sided with palm fronds, hid wooden tables. It was crowded with onlookers and card players. The plunk, plunk sound of a ukulele was heard from somewhere in the background.

Cries of "Jess, Jess," raised above the hot, sweaty crowds surrounding the small, dirt-covered arena as the chickens weighed in and were measured for size. The cocks were matched. Filipino and Portuguese laborers placed verbal bets, shouting "Young Boy!" or "Old Man!" to identify their favorites, and waving collected stacks of bills in their hands. Each owner, his fighting cock under his arm, entered the ring and met with the referee. The chickens pecked at each other. The excitement mounted, and shouts and betting increased.

The handlers moved away from each other and crouched down, holding their fighters back while unsheathing the razor-sharp knives wrapped to each chicken's legs. The referee signaled, and the fight was on. The cocks sparred like two boxers before flying at each other in mortal combat. A hit was made! The blade penetrated deep into the vitals of a chicken called Red. It fell back. The opponent went for an all-out kill. The fight was over.

Money was collected. "Young Boy" picked up his fallen chicken and handed it to an old lady. A boiling pot was waiting out back. The chicken,"Red," would be served for lunch. In this scene, we were transported back in time one hundred, maybe a thousand years. Tuna fit in, and so did I.

Chapter 57

Future shock was upon us and Hawaiian tourism mushroomed overnight into an industry of immense proportions. New hotels and condominiums rose up everywhere in response to the jumbo jets arriving almost hourly, discharging capacity loads of vacationers. The beach services at Fort DeRussy, the Halekulani, and Reef Hotel flourished with this mad influx of tourists, and they began to demand more and more of my time.

New subdivisions and shopping centers turned once-sleepy little towns like Waipahu into mini-complexes of teeming activity. The long, congested drive from Waikiki to the country was beginning to take its toll on me. Traffic cops grew to know my hectic highway routine better than I did; the glove compartment was full of citations.

Barbara and I discussed the difficulties arising from trying to conduct the city business from a North Shore country home. Each played an almost equally important role in my life, yet every day, the barriers between the two seemed to grow. We decided that the best course of action for me to take would be to keep an apartment in town. This way I could devote more time to work and be fresh to enjoy our weekends together in the country. Besides, it would be no big thing for Barbara to pop into Honolulu from time to time, meet me for lunch, shopping, or evenings on the town.

I found a super apartment on the 29th floor of The Ilikai Hotel. We stocked it with food and clothes and, as money was no object, we bought our problems away. A closeness was reestablished with my own family, one I had not enjoyed for years. I saw to it that mother was well taken care of and my brothers found in me a supporting pal they had never really bothered to know.

How we loved our life in the country. Barbara's kids, Anne and David, were blossoming into fine young adults. Barbara was busy all the time, and where once I had been the master chef producing all manner of ethnic dishes and delights, she was rapidly taking over. Even Sunset, our prize Arabian stud, was becoming the talk of Haleiwa. In short: man, I had the world by the tail and I knew it!

"Left hook, David! Left hook! Right cross! You got 'em on the ropes! Go for the midsection! Lefts and rights, lefts and rights! 15 seconds. You got 'em. Don't let 'em get away. Keep punchin', keep punchin', keep punchin'! Aw right, time's up!"

The big heavy bag swung back and forth. We had it attached to an eave on the patio out by the swimming pool. The sun was warm, the breeze refreshing, and David was looking good. He was a lean, hard, tall, wirey blond kid. We worked out like this together at least five days a week. David went to Waialua High School—no easy thing for a rich *haole* kid to do. I was real proud of him. He was holding his own. He'd had a few tough beefs and done damn well.

"Hey, you're looking like a champ, kid. Those combinations are really starting to work for you."

"Yeah, it's starting to feel really good," he said, sweat pouring off his body. David bit at the laces of his glove, the muscles in his shoulders, arms and chest pumped full of blood ripple in the sunlight.

"What are you going to do with the rest of the day?" I asked, half hoping he would include me in his plans.

"A couple of the guys are coming by in a little while, we're going to ride a few waves."

Our house sat right in front of Chun's Reef, a great North Shore surfing spot, and I envied the enthusiasm of youth, the eagerness to test and thrill.

"Okay, that sounds good, but you gotta do one thing for me before your pals arrive. The trees are loaded with bananas, and they're goin' to rot if we don't pick 'em fast. Your mother and I have some people coming over tomorrow, and I want that fruit all ready so they can take some home with them."

"Are you going to get some fish, too?" he asked, putting his gloves away in the cabinet.

"Of course, how're we going to have a party with no fish?"

"Then you want me back by five, huh?"

"Eh, you'll have your fill of surfing by then. Just don't wear yourself out too much."

"Are you kiddin'?" He was acting macho now. "See you at five."

"Better make it quarter to. Now get going on those bananas, or you're going to hold up your guys."

I watched David take off around the side of the house. I hit the big bag a shot with my fist. It felt good and I banged in a few lefts and rights, tossed my shirt on a lounge chair and jumped in the pool.

"Barry!" It was Barbara. She was standing just outside the sliding glass doors that opened off to the pool from the playroom.

"Is that all you've got to do, is just stand there, exposing your beautiful bronze body to the elements?"

Actually I was just drying off from my swim and watching the surfers at Chun's. No more beautiful pasttime in the world, even more so now that girls were into it. There's something about blue water, trim bodies and bikinis I don't think I'll ever be too old to enjoy.

"What do you mean by robbing a hard-working man of a few moments of leisure?" I yelled back.

"I've got a carload of groceries that need putting away, that's what I mean."

I walked across the grass toward her, thinking, the old gal still looks pretty good. Her shorts were tight, adding a very sexy topping to her tan, smooth legs, and I could feel her eyes penetrating through the skin-like nylon of my swimming trunks. And as I stopped by the chair and began to step into my overshorts, she mocked and taunted me. "Killjoy."

"Now who's talking," I said. "I thought your mind was on groceries," and gave her a playful slap on the rear. She reached back and fluttered her fingers across my *uli* and shook her bottom playfully. I grabbed her hips and pulled her ass in tight against me, kissing the back of her neck and feeling my hardness begin to probe the deep, soft crevice between the round mounds of her ass.

"Where's David?" she whispered.

"Gone surfing," I replied, still working on her neck and her ears.

"Then what're we doing here?"

She took my hand and led me through the playroom and into the living room. Water was trickling down the rocks of our indoor waterfall, forming tiny bubbles, which the pop-eyed carp were biting at. "Did you ever fuck in front of a fish?" she mischievously asked.

"Not since this morning," I replied, bringing her close to me.

"Was she exciting?" she asked.

"Fantastic!" I replied.

Her hand slipped down the front of my trunks.

"Big boobs?" Her breathing began to increase. I could feel her heart pounding, and unbuttoned her blouse.

"Pretty good." Now my heart was racing. Her grip became firmer, pulling the skin on my hard-on back and forth. I felt her nipples harden between my fingers. She pulled my tights down and cupped my *uli* between her hands.

"God, I do love your cock, I do, I do."

"I know," I answered. "I know you do."

"Did you love her cunt?"

"I loved it."

"Tell me about it, tell me. Did you kiss it?"

I covered her mouth with mine and we sank down on the deep, rich carpet. Barbara raised her hips and pulled her shorts down past her bottom. Once over her knees she kicked out of them, brought her legs up once again, spreading them in open invitation. I played my uli back and forth between her legs, penetrating ever so gently, then withdrawing back out again. She thrust upwards strongly and we locked deeply together, our bodies moving back and forth to the rhythm of love.

A metallic sliding sound came into the house from outside. It was the huge electric front gate. "Oh, shit!" she exclaimed. "Anne and her boyfriend. I forgot she was bringing him for lunch!"

My trunks were wrapped around my ankles and when I rose up, I almost fell into the pond. Barbara grabbed her shorts and raced for the bedroom, with me hopping awkwardly behind.

"Mom! Barry! It's me! We're here!"

"Be right out, Hon," Barbara answered. "We just got back from the store, and are running a little late."

We were both struggling back into our clothes like little kids almost caught by their parents playing doctor. Barbara checked her face in the mirror and, satisfied with what she saw, left the bedroom to greet the kids. I grabbed a fresh pair of underpants from the drawer and headed for the shower.

Anne's boyfriend was a nice, polite young guy. He was in the service, stationed in Hawaii, and hailed from the deep South. His manner of speech was colored with a deep-rooted tradition of 'Yes, ma'ams' and 'No, sirs', and though he was some years older than Anne, he seemed to treat her with all the gentleness and respect any proud parent could hope for. I had raised Anne and looked upon her as my very own.

"Look what Bob has brought us," Barbara said, holding up a bottle of imported wine as I entered the room.

"It's for lunch," he added. "Anne and I aren't wine drinkers, but I thought you might enjoy it."

"Oh, we will," Barbara replied, clutching the bottle and heading off toward the kitchen. "Entertain Bob, Barry, while Anne and I put some lunch together."

Anne winked at me, got up and followed her mother into the kitchen. I shook hands with Bob, muttering a "Howzit" and sat down with a strange, foreboding feeling. Barbara seemed a bit too eager to whisk that wine away.

"Pardon me?" I said to Bob. "I've been swimming this morning and my ears are still full of water." I had missed his first attempt at starting up a conversation. My mind was in the kitchen.

"Oh, I just asked, sir, how the fishing had been."

At best, this kid and I had difficulties in communicating with each other. We both tried, but aside from Anne, the two of us had very little in common. Without a third party to help us along, there were usually long pauses ending with both of us starting to talk at the same time about the same things.

"There are always plenty of fish out here, and with a net, it's hard to miss," I said.

"A net? Boy, that sounds like something I'd like to see."

"Well, stick around. David and I are going to lay one later this afternoon."

"Sounds great," he said, and silence enveloped us.

"Just make yourself at home, Bob, for a few minutes will you? I just remembered I left some groceries out in the car."

"Can I give you a hand?" he offered.

"No, thanks anyway. It's just a small bag, but I think it's the one with the ice cream in it." I fibbed. I went into the kitchen. The door leading to the carport was open and I could see

Anne picking up a shopping bag off the rear seat of the station wagon. My premonition about the bottle of wine had been well founded, for Barbara had already opened the bottle and a half-filled wine glass was sitting on the kitchen counter.

"Hey, what's with the sauce?" I asked Barbara.

"Now, don't be such a poop and wreck a perfectly innocent afternoon. It's just a glass of wine and I don't want to hurt his feelings. It was a very thoughtful gesture."

Anne came bursting through the door, her face hidden behind two over-loaded bags. I took the drooping sacks from her arms and set them on the counter. She put her arms around me and planted a big kiss on my cheek.

"Oh, it's good to see you. How was your week in town?"

"Very lonely without you," I said.

Anne was such an up-front kid and I did miss her. She seemed to grow more beautiful every weekend.

We had a delicious lunch out on the patio, drank glasses of cold iced tea, and no mention was ever made of the wine. Our house sat about 25 feet up off the sandy beach. At times it was higher, depending on the whims of the tide and ferocity of a sea that could eat a beach away overnight. If you were to stand on the edge of the property, the view was commanding, but addicted as I am to watching waves and currents, I built a lookout platform on top of the property—a crow's nest where I was able to get a bird's-eye view of my beloved ocean. From this choice spot, using binoculars, I could see outside the reef break to the deep water where the lobsters live. When my tastebuds cried out for the sweet, juicy meat of a fresh-boiled lobster, I'd grab my old 12-foot tandem board and follow the swift currents inked clearly in my mind out to the hidden coral reefs I knew so well. I'd tie a line through a hole I had drilled down and tie up to a skeleton branch of coral. The water was always crystal clear, and here and there you could see the antenna-like feelers of the fat bugs protruding from the crusted caverns. One or two light tugs on the spiny spires could bring them out charging mad. A firm grab over the back and it was up to the surface, the tail slapping like fury.

Anne and Bob had decided to watch the laying of the net some other time, and took off for town, giving Barbara and I the opportunity of finishing what we had started earlier in the day. When David came home, he was late, as usual. No matter. There was still plenty of daylight left to do what we had to do.

A late afternoon calm settled over this part of the island. The sun was low in the west, peeking through the coconut palms. A group of young surfer kids were on the beach, drinking beer and playing their guitars. David had our fishing gear spread out over the back lawn and I was up in the lookout, eagerly scanning the sea conditions. A school of fish had turned the surface of the inside waters into a silver-grey maelstrom, zigzagging back and forth in search of smaller prey.

"Hey, David!" I yelled. "There's a big school out there. You ready, brother?"

"Yeah, all set. Just got to make this floater fast."

The float is a big plastic bubble-like affair, filled with a cluster of empty plastic containers. Our objective would be to get the net laid down outside the school of fish before they headed back out for the open sea. The fish would not be able to see the net when it was suspended in the water and would run right into it, trapping themselves in the half-inch mesh.

There had been times when we'd caught three or four

hundred fish. At least 20 or 30 could usually be counted on in one cutting. Our nets were six feet wide, 150 feet long, and cork floats ran across the top, lead weights along the bottom. The nets could not stay in the water overnight, for one of two things would happen: the netted fish would be eaten by moray eels and barricuda, or—and this is a strange phenomenon—somehow, just before sunup, they would find the wherewithal to fight their way free. Our work would be cut out for us until 10 or 11 o'clock that night.

• • •

Sundays were family days in Hawaii. On this one, in particular, the Napoleon household opened its doors to some good friends and North Shore neighbors. Barbara had laid out a bountiful buffet. People arrived bearing gifts of bananas, papayas, sweet fresh corn, cabbages and onions which they had grown, and would leave with kumu and opakapaka wrapped in newspaper, from the catch David and I had brought in the night before.

The tennis court reverberated with the sound of balls meeting gutted strings, screeching rubber soles and the grunts, ohs and ahs of friendly competition. There was laughter from the pool area as a huge man bounced, clown-like, on the diving board and hit the water with a splash that rose 20 feet into the air. I watched a handful of bills change hands across the pool table as an 8 ball plopped into a corner pocket. Every patio chair was filled with a happy guest, and I was the proudest guy on this—or any other—island.

Chapter 58

Monday morning, 5 a.m. The moonlight glistened off the palms and illuminated the driveway, bordered thick with philodendron and hibiscus. I opened the door of my sleek, shiny Mark IV. The interior had not yet lost that new-car smell of machinery and fresh paint mixed with rich leather upholstery. The powerful engine responded to the first turn of the key. The instrument panel and headlights came on, the iron gate slid open, and I was off for another week in the city.

The countryside was still asleep, except for the occasional bedroom light of an early riser. By the time I had reached Waialua, there was a faint glow reflecting over the tops of the Koolau Range, and I knew the plantation workers had begun to stir within the confines of their ramshackle houses. The back road ran up through fields of sugar cane and bisected the barracks and drill fields of Schofield. At the stop sign, I turned right onto Kunia Road. It was desolate at that time of the morning, but in a few short hours it would be alive with truckloads of pineapples from the farms of Del Monte and

Dole. In no time, the speedometer crept up past 70 and, being cop-wary, I kept one eye on the rear view mirror and the other on the road. I noticed headlights fast coming up behind me and eased my foot back off the accelerator. As the car drew up close enough for me to ascertain that it was not the law, I stepped back down on the gas. The other car hung tight on my tail, though, never giving up an inch. I was doing 80 now, and whoever it was, they were still with me. Daylight dawned at the top of a rise. I doused my headlights and the guy behind me did the same. He was driving a Thunderbird and obviously wanted to play.

Probably some hot jet jockey looking for a warmup. Okay, brother, you're on! 80 ... 85 ... 90 ... no let up. I hit the brakes, my tires squealing through an S turn in the road, and then pushed right back up to speed. 95 now, and then it happened. A whistling siren bust through the sound of speed, and a flashing blue light of the highway patrol invaded my car.

Oh, shit! I said to myself, and I let up off the gas.

The cop crossed over the double line and waved the guy behind me off the road. In what seemed like a split second, he was beside me, too, his mouth opening and closing like a bug-eyed ventriloquist dummy whose string was being yanked by an orangutan. I pulled over on the soft shoulder, my motor still running, and watched what was taking place through the rear view mirror. The cop got out of his car, pulled his nightstick out of its sheath and swaggered up to the window of the Thunderbird. He yanked the young guy out of the car and spread-eagled him across the front fender. When I saw this, I pulled out, leaving them in a cloud of dust. *One ticket like that's enough for any cop*, I though to myself. *Hell, he didn't even have* time to get my number. I'd be off this road and lost in the Kam Highway traffic before he could get back into the car. I was wrong. Dead wrong. He came down on me like a Harley Davidson chasing a Moped.

"Get outta that car, you fucker!" he screamed. His .38 looked bigger than both of us. He searched through the trunk, looked under the seats, through the glove compartment and then called into headquarters on his radio.

"I got a black Mark IV, license number 8E2803, operator's name Napoleon, Barry, Kam Highway address. Give me a readout."

He hooked his mike back on the receiver and started in on me, slapping at my pants, butt, sides and chest. I wondered if he was going to unzip my fly when a staccato voice blared out over his radio.

He picked up the two-way mike once again in his hand, and after haggling back and forth with headquarters was apparently satisfied that he did not have a fugitive or suspected murderer on his hands. In a deep voice with a heavy Island accent, he read me up one side and down the other, writing all the time and finally running out of space recording my violations. I signed the ticket, carefully reading the part about it not being an admission of guilt, only a promise to appear.

• • •

The court clerk called my name and spewed forth the endless list of charges. The judge stared down at me and said, "On this note, I'm going to have to recess the court for 15 minutes. Mr. Napoleon, can I see you in my chambers?"

The doors closed behind as the judge turned to me.

"Nappy, what's the matter with you? You gone crazy or something?"

The judge and I had gone to school together. He was like family to me.

"You know Kunia Road?" I said, and he nodded. "In the morning, there's no cars there, and this *haole* guy comes up behind me and wants to play. It was no big thing. We were doing 80, 85 and get pulled over. So I accept that. But when I see this guy coming up with a big nightstick I think, *Hey, I got two choices: I can bust him, which is bad, or leave, which is bad, too, but not quite so bad, I don't think.*"

The judge looked at me and nodded and then said, "But the report here says you did stop the second time."

"Yeah. But this time he had a gun," I said.

"Okay, Barry. Tell you what I'm going to do about this thing, and this time you're going to follow orders. I'm going to order you outta here and I never want to see you in this court for anything like this again. You understand?"

"I understand," I said.

"You know, we Hawaiians are losing enough ground as it is. We got to stick together, take 'em on. But this kind of action ain't the way. Okay?"

"Okay."

We shook hands and I left the judge's chambers. When I walked out on the hallway the arresting officer was there, a big *hapa-haole* guy, giving me the stink-eye.

Chapter 59

Once a year, the Jaycees of Haleiwa would put on a carnival, the Haleiwa Sea Spree. It would kick off with the biggest little parade in the world, right down the main street of town, which was also the main artery around the island, the Kamehameha Highway. The whole thing would take about 15 minutes, but traffic would back up at both ends of the parade route. Tour bus drivers would moan and groan about the delay and threaten to have the parade shut down each year. There were rides and slides, canoe races, 100-yard horse sprints, art and craft displays, entertainers, and something for everybody if they're young at heart. Barbara and I always took the kids. We bought a bunch of carnival script and we ate everything in sight. This year was no exception, and I wished with all my heart and soul that it could go on like this forever. But life must change. Nothing stays the same forever, and I felt that this would probably be the last Spree together as a family unit. David was almost a man, and as I watched Anne and her boyfriend walking hand in hand, it was apparent that she was getting ready to leave the nest any time. What I didn't know was the shot aimed at every father's heart had already been fired and was winding through the air, waiting for an opportune moment to strike.

One evening, a few weeks later, Barbara and I had just returned home from eating dinner at the Proud Peacock, a favorite restaurant of ours at the foot of Waimea Falls. Anne and Bob were waiting for us.

"Bob has something he'd like to ask you," Anne said.

"Mr. and Mrs. Napoleon? I love your daughter very much and she loves me. We would like to ask your permission to get married."

I looked at Barbara and she looked back at me. Her eyes filled with tears, she nodded a silent yes, rushed up to Anne and hugged her.

"Bob, you have our blessings."

We sent out over 500 wedding invitations. Mrs. Hahn arrived a week early and when we met her at the plane she was positively radiant. She handed her daughter a blank check, saying, "Kids, we've got a lot of work yet to do." Her enthusiasm was contagious. I caught fire immediately.

"David, you watch out for your grandmother's luggage," I barked, and then stepped over to an airport telephone and placed a long-distance call to Alameda, California. My brother Walter answered the phone.

"Walter," I said, bubbling over with enthusiasm, "You get your wedding invitation?"

"Yeah, we have it," he answered.

"Well, you and Rhoda gotta drop whatever it is you're doing and come over here and help us with Anne's wedding. Can you manage a few days off? I'm at the airport right now.

Just say yes, and I'll wire your tickets. We're gonna have the biggest damn luau you ever saw!"

Rhoda picked up the other phone. "You hear what Barry just said?" I heard Walter exclaim to Rhoda.

"How could I? I just got on the line," she answered back.

"Well, we ain't got time to repeat it," he said. "Just start packing your bag. We're gonna put on a luau!"

"Call Mother," I shouted. "She's coming, too."

• • •

The celebration started three days before the ceremony. I couldn't believe Barbara's mother. She was cutting salmon, wrapping lau laus, calling florists, buying things for everybody. Rhoda and Walter were real pros at the catering game. There was no doubt in my mind about the kind of affair they would put on. The entertainment fell on my shoulders, and I got the best. Anne and her mother were like peas in a pod, preparing for the biggest day in her daughter's life.

Our back yard was more beautiful than any movie set. An altar of flowers was set up on the back lawn with palms, white sands, and blue sky and sea for a backdrop. A large tent enclosed the tennis court. The orchestra would set up there. Chinese lanterns were everywhere, and white-jacketed parking attendants lined up in the drive, awaiting the first arrivals. The service was solemn and brief. There wasn't a dry eye among over 500 people when my brother Walter sang *Ke Kali Ne Ou* with my sister-in-law, Nalani, at the end of the ceremony. Cocktails were served on the patio, and guests mingled on the wide walks around the pool area as Genoa Keawe and her musicians filled the air with old Hawaiian standards. Knife dancers and hula girls performed after dinner, giving way to Nalani Olds from the Kahala Hilton and the full orchestra. Anne and her husband danced the first dance before the large crowd. I squeezed Barbara's hand, offered her my arm, and we moved out onto the floor to the applause and well-wishes of everyone, and soon the dance floor was packed.

"Happy, momma?" I asked, going into a series of turns.

"Happier than I've ever been in my whole life," and her cheek pressed close to mine.

I am not, nor have I ever been, a big drinker. But that night, as is any father's right when he gives his daughter away, I toasted away the past and drank to the future. Unfortunately, so did Barbara. We had hired a small group of young hippie-type girls from the Sunset Beach area to help wait tables and clean up. We saw to it that they appeared neat and fresh. Barbara helped do up the hair, adding a fresh flower here and there, and outfitting them in colorful muumuus.

After Anne and her husband had departed and people's refinement began to lose its sheen, I noticed one of the girls—she must have been six feet tall—getting playful with Barbara in the kitchen. Every time anyone would enter with a tray of dishes or glasses, their mood seemed to change. Then when they were alone again they stood close, touching here and there, laughing as though they had some private joke going on between them. But I was getting drunk, and so was Barbara. So were we all.

The party was over, the last houseguest had gone, and a blanket of calm settled over the house once again. And I went back to the city.

• • •

On Tuesday, a friend called me to set up a Wednesday golf date. I hadn't played since before the wedding and was anxious to try out my new putter. Then I remembered I'd left the bugger at Haleiwa, so I decided to go home for lunch, spend the rest of the day working around the house, and planned to come back to town early the next morning.

There was an old car parked in the driveway when I got home. I opened the front door of the house and called out, "Barbara?" No answer. "Barbara!" I went into the bedroom, opened the closet and got out my new putter, but still no answer. Well, maybe she's out in back. I called her name once again from the pool area, and she came scurrying around the side of the house from the direction of the servants' quarters.

"What're you doing home?" she asked. It was more an exclamation than a question.

"Forgot my putter," I said, holding the club up in front of me, and added, "How about some lunch? I'm starved."

"Yes, master. Anything else your humble servant can get for you?"

"Hey, what's with you? All I asked for was some lunch," I said, kind of irritated at the tone of her voice.

"A thousand pardons, but I was just about to go to the store."

Aw, it must be her period, I thought. No big thing.

"Terrific. I'll go with you, huh?"

We piled into the station wagon, and I thought I picked up the faint scent of booze on her breath, but she didn't appear to have been drinking and the wind quickly cleansed the air.

"Whose old car is that in the driveway?" I asked.

"I don't know. Probably belongs to some friend of David's. He left early this morning."

When we got home from the store, the car was gone, and Barbara suddenly seemed less anxious.

"You remember that hippie girl that came to work for us the night of the wedding?" I asked, putting the finishing touches on the macaroni salad I was making.

"Yeah, I think so. Why do you ask?" she came back a bit too nonchalantly.

"Oh, I don't know. It just looked to me like you were getting pretty friendly."

"What were you doing? Checking on me? For Chrissakes, that pisses me off! Anne's getting married and you think all I've got to do is shine on some young chick. Boy! I put my foot into it this time. Well, fuck it! Things were going real good around here 'til you had to come home!"

"Then I'll leave," I said.

"I wish you would. And take that goddamned macaroni salad with you!"

Shit, I thought to myself, as I climbed the grade up out of Haleiwa. *I wish I hadn't gone home.* And the thought of that old car and who it really belonged to loomed larger and larger in my mind.

• • •

I had just climbed into bed that evening when the phone rang. "Hello," I said.

"Are you still speaking to me?" It was Barbara.

"I said hello, didn't I?"

"Well, I'm sorry I was such an old bitch today," she said. There was a long pause, the last two words, 'bitch today' seemed to slur together then. "But I guess it was just the aftershock of the wedding and all."

"Uh, huh," I muttered. No doubt about it now, she was drinking.

"Anyhow, lover," she continued, "I was working in the yard today. Shit, there was so fuckin' much to do, and with you gone so much and all…" Another long pause. "I hired a gardener."

"Well, what's wrong with David?" I asked. "He's supposed to be helping out around the place."

"Aw, that independent little fucker. He's at that age. You know what I mean?"

Well, I didn't know what she meant, but I hardly thought this was the appropriate time to bring up what the hell the kid was doing with his time. I'd handle that myself later.

"Okay, you hired a gardener. Great. I'm happy. Now what else is new?"

"Nuthin', except I thought you might like to know about it and interview her, tell her what you expect."

"Her?" I questioned. "You got a girl gardener?"

"What's the matter? You got somethin' 'gainst girls? I always thought you liked girls."

"No, I mean I do. I mean, no, I got nothing against girls, yes I do like 'em. Who knows better than you?"

"Thass what I like to hear," she said, her talk beginning to cloud up even more. "Anyway, what I want you to do is talk to her. I told her you'd meet her at the golf course around seven in the morning."

"I'll be there," I said.

"Oh, and one more thing, be nice to her, huh? Cuz I need her out here. Okay?"

"Okay."

Boy, I thought. *That's a lead line if ever there was one.*

"Now, I'll let you go back to sleep. You gonna be home on Friday?"

"I'll be home. Good night, Barbara."

"G'night."

• • •

I got down to the Ala Wai Golf Course at 6:30 the next morning, took a table in the rear of the dining room facing the main entrance, and ordered breakfast. At about five minutes of seven, this good-looking young chick came walking in the door, long blonde hair, about 5'5", dressed in white shorts, blouse and sandals. I followed her as she walked up to the girl at the cash register. They both looked over in my direction and then this tender young thing came walking up to me.

"Mr. Napoleon?" She was well poised and direct.

"Yes," I answered.

"My name is Clair, and your wife asked me to talk to you about the gardening job."

"You're a gardener?" I asked, incredulously.

"Yes, I am," she replied assuredly.

"Hey, sit down here a minute. We got to talk this one over."

She pulled a chair out from the table and sat down, crossing a pair of legs as shapely as I've seen in a long time.

"Is there something wrong?" she asked suddenly, losing her self-assurance.

"No, nothing's wrong. You just don't look like any gardener

I've ever seen before. How old are you?"

"Nineteen."

"You from around here?"

"Yes. I can give you references if you want," she said.

"Hey, I don't need references."

"Well, I came prepared to tell you anyway, since the job includes room and board."

"It does?" This was news to me.

"Well, that's what your wife said."

"If that's what she said, it must be so. Go on, tell me more."

"Well, I graduated last year from Punahou. My father's a doctor—"

"Hold it," I said. "I don't mean to interrupt, but there's something I don't understand. What're you doing seeking employment as a gardener?"

She seemed taken aback by that question, blunt as it was. I think I caught her off guard. But she fired right back, "It's because of my boyfriend. He lives in Pupukea and I want to be near him."

"I see," I replied. "Well, looks like I just got myself a new gardener."

Chapter 60

Love, the unbridled kind, can be a tenuous affair, particularly in an area like the North Shore. Every day, healthy, good-looking kids from beaches all over the world congregate to do their thing. Clair's romantic dreams soon came crashing down when her boyfriend rode a Sunset Beach wave behind a little surfer girl from Sydney, Australia. She turned to Barbara for consolation. Our new gardener had already begun to fill a void left by Anne, and they became good companions. Barbara gave her the run of the place, the use of the pool, the tennis court, even catered to her vegetarian whims.

My wife's mid-week junkets into the city grew less frequent. Her drinking, at least on the weekends, was increasing. We quarreled almost constantly. Soon, she quit coming to town altogether.

One night, after another sluggish telephone conversation with Barbara, I went up to the bar at the Top if the Ilikai, a swinging singles kind of place. The music was loud, the dance floor crowded, and a night's companionship was never more than one or two drinks away. I met a girl. We volleyed back and forth with the usual preliminaries and discovered that we were neighbors, if such a thing is possible in a big place like the Ilikai. She was just coming off a divorce, had a baby still in diapers, and was staying, temporarily, with her mother. We danced, got jostled by the crowd, lost our places at the bar, and decided to continue this thing someplace where we could hear ourselves talk.

We went downstairs, bought a bottle of whiskey, and took it back up to my apartment. She proceeded to tell me what a rat her husband had turned out to be, how miserable her life had been, all the kind of stuff I didn't want to hear. To top it off, the more she talked, the more she drank.

"Hey, you better take it easy with that stuff," I said.

"Why? I'm in the mood to get drunk. I don't have to drive home."

Well, the hell with this, I thought, so I got up, went into the bedroom and began taking off my clothes. If I wasn't gonna get laid, at least I wouldn't lose any more sleep over it. I was sitting on the bed, in my shorts, taking off my shoes, when, drink in hand, she appeared in the doorway.

"You men are all the same." I looked up. "Expect women to go to bed with you, just like that! Well, not with me you won't!" She dropped her glass on the floor and raised her fist. "Just you try and see where it gets you!"

"Get outta here," I said, "before I do try." And I stood up, glaring ferociously.

"You're crazy!" she said, and ran out the door.

There was no salvation in this kind of action, so I began to cut my stays in the city a day short, using a renewed interest in Thursday afternoon polo out at Mokuleia as an excuse for wanting to go home. On this particular Thursday, I took a nasty spill off my horse, wrenched my back, and twisted the hell out of my thumb. I wrapped it in ice to take the swelling down, walked to my car while bent 45 degrees from the waist up, and called it a day.

When I got home, there was a new Ford Pinto blocking the driveway and music was blaring out the open door in Clair's room. I hobbled up the path to the doorway. Barbara, Clair, and an attractive young woman I'd never seen before were drinking whiskey sours and cackling over the off-key shoutings of some acid rock maniac. The two girls were sprawled out on the bed, sharing an ashtray.

"Well, look who's here!" Barbara exclaimed, laid back in a big chair. She looked me up and down. It wasn't hard to tell I was in pain. "What the hell happened to you?"

"Fell off my horse," I replied, and looked over at the two figures on the bed for some sign of reaction. None was forthcoming. I felt as though I had just blundered into the women's locker room. Barbara spoke up.

"Barry, say hello to Mary. She's an old school chum of Clair's, came to see how the natives live on this side of the island."

"Hello, Mary," I said, painfully nodding from a neck that was growing stiffer by the second.

"Hi," was the reply.

"Mary's married to an architect," Barbara cut through the ice that was beginning to form in the room. "She has two kids. Would you believe it? Hardly looks like more than a kid herself, doesn't she?"

Barbara and Clair raised their eyebrows in unison and giggled at one another. I excused myself, declining the offer of a good stiff drink to cure what ailed me. What I needed more was an ice pack for my thumb and a good hot bath.

The steaming water was drawing the aches and pains from my body. I was laid out flat in the big tub, immersed up to my ears, when the door opened and Barbara walked into the bathroom.

"Party's over?" I asked.

"I think it's just beginning," was the conspiritorial reply.

"What do you mean?"

"Mary's going to spend the weekend and the two of them are getting ready to go have dinner at the Proud Peacock."

She knelt down by the tub, placed her elbows on the edge, resting her chin in her hands. "What do you think?" she said.

"About what?" I answered.

"Those two out there, Clair and her friend."

"What's to think?"

Now, I knew Barbara well enough to know that she was about to tell me something.

"Well, I was just getting ready to take a little nap this afternoon," she said, drawing one finger back and forth in the water. "When I heard all this splashing and carrying on in the pool. You know me, I don't like to miss anything, so I peeked out the window. Mary was chasing Clair around the deck and dove in the water after her. They were screaming like a couple of teenyboppers."

"So," I commented. "What's the big thing? They're not much older than that, either one of them."

"Well, for one thing, they didn't have anything on, and for

another, when Mary caught up to her in the shallow end, they started playing with each other," she reached down and took hold of me.

"You want to tell me about it?" I said.

"Oh, yes," she replied, rubbing me up and down. She slipped out of her muumuu and sat on top of me in the tub. My stiff neck suddenly left me and went someplace else.

• • •

Sunday night, Barbara and I had dinner together at the Haleiwa Sands. I was bone tired when we returned home. My back was still bothering me and I went straight to bed. About two o'clock in the morning, I woke up with a start to the sound of shots. James Cagney was being gunned down on the top of a gas storage tank. "Look ma, the top of the world!" he shouted, riddled with bullets. He fired a shot into the tank and the whole TV screen exploded. Barbara was lying next to me, oblivious to Cagney's—or anyone else's—fate, so I eased myself up out of bed and turned off the set in the middle of a Honolulu Ford commercial. The title of the old Cagney film was driving me crazy as I stumbled into the kitchen for a drink of water. *White Heat*, I suddenly thought. *That was it*.

The thought came to me in the middle of a large gulp. Satisfied that my powers of retention were still in working order, I set the glass down by the sink and noticed a ray of light coming from the servants' quarters. Barbara's description of the two young nymphs aroused my curiosity. I snuck outside, crept up to the window. The curtains were drawn but I could hear soft voices and giggles.

I went around to the back of the room. There was another

window, but it was too high to peer into, even though the blinds were half-open. But what I was hearing spurred me on, and I climbed up in the papaya tree.

Clair and Mary were on the bed. They were locked in a tight embrace, caressing each other with knowing tenderness. Clair reached up and took what looked like a small bottle of coconut oil off the dresser. She poured a small quantity in her hand and offered the same to Mary. Their hands slid over each other's boobs, stomachs, *okoles* and legs, slick fingers explored every orifice. I felt shots of adrenaline explode in my stomach. Pandora's box was opening before my eyes.

• • •

At 5 a.m., I left again for town. I skipped polo practice that next Thursday and stayed in town over the weekend to play in a golf tournament. I called home and asked Barbara to join me, and immediately wished I hadn't. She was drunk. There was music and laughter in the background.

"What the hell's going on out there?" I asked.

"Clair's old boyfriend just stopped by and we're having a little party."

"Who else is there?" I demanded.

"Just little old me and Mary."

The following week, I stayed at the Ilikai until Saturday. I had not spoken to Barbara in all that time. It was after five when I arrived home. Barbara was alone and drinking.

"This is a hell of a marriage," I said. "Jeezus, what's going on?"

"You said it, I didn't," was her reply.

"And you're doing it," I came back. "To me, yourself, and

everybody else around this place, as near as I can figure out."

"Are you looking for a true confession, lover boy?"

"If that's what you're offering. I'll take anything."

"All right, big man," she looked at me defiantly, and poured herself another drink. "Sit your ass down." She raised the glass to her lips and took a big swallow. "My drinking bugs you, doesn't it?"

"Yeah, it bugs the hell out of me," I replied.

"Good. Now, how does this grab you? You remember the night you called and we were having a little party out here? Well, things got to going so good I let Clair and her guy sleep in the big house, and I spent the night out there." She toasted her glass in the direction of the maid's room. "With Mary." She took another long drink, her head moving unsteadily back and forth.

"Are you through, Barbara?"

"No, I'm not through, you sonofabitch. I'm just getting started. Cuz the next night, the very next night I was sittin' right here on my very own couch, watching my very own TV with Clair, when she kisses me right here, on the lips. You like that one? Do you?"

I just sat there looking at her. And she continued.

"Well, I don't really care one way or the other, 'cuz we've been lovin' each other ever since!"

I got up and walked out of the house.

• • •

Tuna was sitting on his front porch, sharpening some knives when I arrived.

"You goin' to the chicken fights tomorrow, brother?" he said.

"Depends," I said, as I ambled up the old wooden steps and sat down next to him.

"I got a good red chicken, could make us a lotta money."

I nodded my head. My mind was a thousand miles away. Tuna knew I didn't feel like talking, and it didn't matter. He continued sharpening his knives while I watched the sun fall out of the sky. I ate dinner at Tuna's that night and drove back to Haleiwa about nine o'clock. The station wagon was gone, but David's Corvette was parked in the garage. Maybe it was better that way. I could go to bed without another flare-up.

I called for David when I entered the house. There was no answer. He was not in his room. No one was around. The dogs hadn't even barked. I went outside and checked the kennels. The gates were open. Goddamn it all! They could be in Wailua right now!

I knocked gently on Clair's door, though I felt like breaking it down.

"Yes, who is it?"

"It's me, Barry."

"What do you want? I'm trying to go to sleep."

"I want to talk to you. Now!"

"Jes' a minute. I have to put something on." The light went on, she opened the door, wearing a thin cotton nightie. Obviously, she slept in the nude.

"Where are Barbara and David?" I asked.

"I think they went to dinner and to a show," she replied.

"Did you know the dogs were out?" I said, brushing past her and entering the room.

"That's not my bag," she said, turning to face me. "I'm paid to garden."

"That's not all you're paid to do," I said, and I grabbed the hem of her nightie.

"Sorry, I'm not that kind."

"You like girls better? Barbara, maybe?" I asked.

"Screw you. You don't know what you're talking about!"

"Don't I? You calling my wife a liar?"

It hit her like a slap in the face. "She told you?"

"You better believe she told me! Now, get your ass in gear. Let's go find those dogs!"

Chapter 61

There was an old, run-down, one-story building on the corner of Palama and School Streets. It was decorated with graffiti and the windows were boarded up to discourage vandals and burglars. It was my office, warehouse, and repair shop. The cement floor was covered with fine particles of spun glass and beaded drops of hardened plastic from the sanding and glassing of a thousand surfboards. A canoe hull balanced atop two scarred and paint-splattered sawhorses. The side walls were cluttered with tools hanging from rusted nails. There were rolls of fiberglass, and a large color photograph of a nude girl laying on a bear rug with her legs kicking playfully in the air took up three-quarters of an outdated calendar. It was tacked onto a four by four support beam over a finger-stained yellow wall telephone and offered the user a close up front view of a pink vagina.

Surfboards of every size and state of disrepair were stacked against the walls next to paddles, *amas,* and rudders. Two bare, 200-watt lightbulbs hung from crossbeams supporting a rust-tinted, corregated iron roof that cracked incessantly on hot days and reverberated like bullets hitting on a tin drum when it rained.

My private office was sealed off from all the noise and grime by bare, unfinished plywood forming a small square box just off the front entrance. I had an old window from a condemned building built into the side so I could observe my boys at work while seated behind a paper-cluttered, time-ravaged desk. There was a small bed for emergencies, and a faded green cotton rug on the floor. One cigar usually lasted me about a week, and it rested in an ashtray, ready to be lit, puffed on a couple of times, and snuffed out until the smoking urge came on me again.

Two heavy doors, chipped and dented, led from the workroom to the outside yard. Twenty-five years of beach equipment was jammed under makeshift sheds, lean-tos, and weathered canvas tarps. The yard was bordered on one side by a Chinese market and on the remaining sides by a bowed, 12-foot sheet metal fence. The rear yard belonged to my watchdogs: two ex-convicts from the Oahu prison. They slept here, rent-free. It was a real open-air affair, a couple of shanties boarded up for privacy with cots inside. Each used a faded curtain for a front door, a wash basin and toilet built onto the outside of the building for use by all of us. The shower was an exposed pipe with a small head attached to it.

It was hot in my office that day. There was no one there but me and the mosquitoes. I rummaged through a junk-laden drawer and found my last mosquito punk. I put it on the far corner of the desk and lit it. The sweet-smelling fumes funneled up towards the ceiling, spreading out when they were caught by the warm draft that seeped in from the outside between the cracks of the walls and the ceiling. The mosquitoes would all be dead soon. Perhaps a couple of strong puffs from my three-day-old cigar butt would help hasten the job. I lit another match and took a few quick drags. *It's too hot for cigars.* A thick stack of bills stared back at me like a pack of hungry dogs. *Let 'em wait. I don't want to think about this junk on a Saturday afternoon.* I picked up the telephone, dialed 543-3211, and listened. "At the tone, the time will be … 12:41 and 30 seconds." I hadn't been home in ten days.

• • •

I got out of the car and walked around the side of the house, picking up fallen coconuts and an unopened, soggy edition of last week's newspaper. The gardens and yards hadn't been touched. As I made my way around to the patio, I could see into the house. Barbara and Clair were on the couch making love. I felt like a guy seated in the doctor's office, looking at his x-rays and blindsided by the words, "I'm sorry, there's nothing we can do. It's inoperable. The cancer has spread too far."

• • •

"Sunset!" I called out. The big horse turned around at the sound of my voice and ambled over to me. He snuggled up against my shoulders and I brought his nose up against my cheek.

"You miss me, pal?" His head bobbed up and down as though he actually understood.

"Sure you do. I know. Tell you what. We're gonna fix you up, make you look presentable, then we're gonna take us a long ride."

The mountains were green and fresh with life. Sunset wanted to run and I let him go. He galloped like no horse I'd ever ridden before. It was like riding on air, and he responded to the slightest touch on the reins. In no time, we were in Tuna Sampaio's territory. We stopped on top of a ridge and looked down into the valley below. And there he was, good old Tuna, surrounded by a group of his paniolos. *God, it'd be good to talk story with a man like him.*

"Tuna!" I shouted, and heard my voice echo back to me. I directed my attention to the horse. "Come on, Sunset! Let's go!" And off we flew down the hill.

• • •

It was after dark when I got back to the house. Barbara's car was still in the driveway. I pulled in alongside, left the motor running, and sat there for a minute. I could hear the dogs barking inside, raising a terrible ruckus.

"Quiet down, you no-good mutts!" I yelled, as I walked toward the house. Mutts? Hell, we had three Great Danes and an Airedale! The barks turned to whines as I put the key in the door. "Shut up in there!" They knew it was me.

When the door opened, two Great Danes jumped up on me. I felt like I was hit with 300 pounds. Their force spun me halfway around the entry hall before I could slap them down. In the process, I stepped in a great crusty cake of Great Dane shit. It caused my foot to slide out from under me, creating a skid mark of foul-smelling crap. I turned on the entry light, cursing like a sailor, and tossed the dogs and my shoes outside the door.

When I turned around, closing the door behind me, I

saw Barbara. She was passed out on the couch. the front room looked like a cyclone had hit it. Clothes, newspapers, halfempty glasses and plates scattered here and there. The bedroom was in shambles, dirty sheets and pillowcases. The dogs had completely annihilated one chair, the screen door was torn. I stepped over a pile of dirty clothes and returned to the living room. There were still three or four shots left in a Vodka bottle on the coffee table in front of Barbara. I poured the last dregs into her hair and stormed out of the house.

The first thing Monday morning, I called a cleaning service.

Chapter 62

"I think the time has come for us to sit down together and have a long talk," I said to Barbara over the phone. "Yes," she answered. "I have to agree with you. When will you be coming out?"

It was nine o'clock in the morning and she was sober, a completely different personality. "The sooner, the better," I said. "I can be there in an hour."

"Good, I'll look forward to seeing you then."

I rehearsed what I was going to say all the way out to Haleiwa. *You've let that little bitch Clair take over the house. She's quit cleaning the yard, she tells you what to do, bitches about what you've fixed for dinner. What's going on in your head? We don't need her, and I'll tell her so. Now your drinking has got to stop. If you need help, then let's get it.*

All of my practiced lines fell on deaf ears. A person can drink a lot of booze in an hour, and that's what Barbara had done. I knew her pattern well: just one little drink to ease the tension, followed by a second and a third.

"You really didn't have to come out here to lay all that bullshit on me, you know," she said.

"Barbara, what's the use? What's the fuckin' use?" I went outside, disgusted and disappointed, and climbed up in my lookout. That seemed to be the last place for me in this house. But even that sanctuary was soon invaded. Clair—that fucking brash kid Clair—was coming up the stairs. I couldn't believe it!

"I don't think you should talk to Barbara like you do," she said.

"What're you telling me?" I shot back. "Go fuck yourself. I'd tell you to go fuck Barbara but you ain't got the equipment for it!"

"We happen to love each other, but I don't suppose a person like you can understand that."

"Well, I understand this," I said. "This is still my house, no matter what you think. One more fuckin' word outta' you and I'm going to come down on you like a ton of bricks!"

I jumped down off the tower and stormed into the house.

"Barbara!" I shouted. "You can take that kid and you can have her! I'm through!"

I made one last trip back to Haleiwa. I didn't call and tell her I was coming, I just appeared. Early. No booze, just talk. Straight talk.

"Barbara, I want a divorce. There's nothing left of this marriage anymore."

"I guess it ended quite a while ago, didn't it?" she said.

"I don't think there's any use makin' a big thing about it. The only one that benefits from that is the attorney."

"That's one thing we do agree on," she said.

"Look," I said. "I don't want anything from this marriage.

Why don't we make an appointment with that lawyer, Amona. Get him to prepare the necessary papers and we'll go in and sign them. We can draw up our own deal on the house later. Half to you and half to me. Fair enough?"

"Fair enough," she said.

We stood there, facing one another in the living room of our beautiful house. Two people with everything, and yet nothing.

"Good-bye, Barbara," I said.

"Good-bye, Barry."

• • •

The next time I saw Barbara was in the lawyer's office.

"Now, I don't think there's any need for a problem here," he said. "I'm sure we can come to terms that will be fair and equitable to both parties concerned under the circumstances."

"You bet your ass we can, pal," I said. "I'm only asking one thing, and that's out."

"That's it?" he asked, making an effort to mask his surprise.

"That's it!"

Chapter 63

K's Fountain up in Kapahulu was nothing more than a hole in the wall. It was a mom and pop operation. They opened up at 6 a.m. and served six stools that were always occupied until they closed their doors sometime after two o'clock in the afternoon. My breakfast, as usual, was nothing short of terrific. The cook always put an extra scoop of rice and macaroni salad on my plate to go along with the eggs. I left a tip that was larger than my bill.

Outside the Fountain, I stopped by the newspaper vending machine to read the headlines in the Honolulu Advertiser.

"Hey, Nappy."

I looked up, answering, "Hey, Menehune. Howzit, brah?"

"You still livin' in Haleiwa?"

"Back on dis side now."

"Oh, das good, huh?"

"Da bes' ting for me, pal."

"You see Bobby lately?"

"I'm jus' on my way ovah to see him."

"Kahala Hilton, yeah? Hey, you be sure to say hello to him for me, huh?"

"I'll do that, brother."

Good old Menehune. Not a tooth left in his head, and he was still working on the beach at the Royal.

Bobby Krewson had now had the beach concession at the Kahala Hilton. His hair had had turned gray, but the flashing eyes and the ever-present infectious smile were a part of Bobby that never grew old. He was sitting at a table out by the beach playing backgammon with one of the hotel guests. The sun beat down and I thought to myself, *If this guy doesn't move into the shade or call a finish to the game pretty soon, he's going to go up in smoke!* Bobby had been on the beach so long, he was impervious to ultraviolet rays.

Not wanting to disturb them, for I knew this was a lucrative side part to Bobby's job, I started to walk out on a man-made coconut island that the hotel had plopped in the bay to give the guests a little more fodder for their Canon cameras.

"Barry, come ovah heah! I want you to meet a friend of mine!" Bobby never was one to ignore a pal, no matter what he was into. He introduced me to a guy from Beverly Hills that had something to do with real estate developments and tax shelters. *Hmmm*, I thought. *Just our type of guy.*

"Don't let me disturb your game," I said.

"Aw, no brother," Bobby was quick to answer. "We just finished and Mr. Feinberg has got to catch his plane. We settle up when you're ready to go, huh, Mr. Feinberg?"

Feinberg looked like he hoped that Bobby would be someplace else when the time came, but said he would stop by the stand later, and then left Bobby and I together, smiling knowingly at each other over the open, sun-bleached backgammon set.

"Just like the good ole days, huh, Barry?" Bobby said. And it was. How many times we had looked at each other in just this way after hoodwinking the hell out of some pompous tourist who thought he knew all the answers?

"Gee, it's good to see you," he said. "It's been too long, you know. We're not kids anymore, time's flying by. We ought to get together more, you know?"

"I know, Bobby," I said. "A couple of old warhorses like us, we still got a lot of fight left, huh?"

"Fo' sure, brother, that's fo' sure! Now tell me," he continued, "what's going on with you? Rumors been flying all over dis place your marriage is *pau*, huh?"

"Eh, a thing of the past now, Bobby," I said.

"You feel like talkin' about it?" he said. "I'm still the best listener, you know."

"Only that I lost a big part of something inside me. I can understand losing out to another guy, but not a woman—and a young punk at that! She really cut my balls off, Bobby!"

He looked at me a moment, compassionately. "Hey! But we're fighters, you and me, da kine come-back kids. You remember that one time I got mixed up with the Major's wife, and he was gon' shoot me and da bugga come down to da beach, wavin' da kine big .45?" Bobby started to laugh. "And I hid out in da country for two weeks? No money or clothes or nuttin'?"

"Yeah," I added, beginning to laugh myself. "And then what about that other time, with the wife of the biggest department store owner in the world? Tell me how you suffered, you bugga!"

"But that went sour, too. Then how you think I felt, huh? And look at your bes' friend now," he continued. "I got my own house in Hawaii Kai, couple new kids, new wife, beeg kine important business here at da bes' hotel on da Island, and jes' leesten to dis. I got my own kine accountant, tells me how good I'm doing."

When I left Bobby and got back into my car, I felt I was ready to go fifteen rounds. I slipped the parking attendant a couple of extra bucks, turned up the radio and headed back to town on Kahala Avenue.

"Aku's Weather Report," the voice on the radio exclaimed, "calls for mostly sunny skies with the chance of brief mauka showers and light to moderate trades. High temperatures in downtown Honolulu should reach 84 degrees, dropping down to a low tonight of about 72."

Kahala turned into Diamond Head Road. *Might as well take the scenic route*, I thought. *It's a beautiful day*. I turned the dial.

"You're listening to KCCN 1420 AM, your Hawaiian music station," the voice on the radio continued. "Let's start off this segment of the Crash Kealoha show with the lovely voice of Melveen Leed singing *The Sands of Waikiki*."

I was fast approaching the Diamond Head Light House, the ocean was an incredible shade of blue. Waves were breaking with beautiful form and I was singing right along with the radio at the top of my voice. Jeezus, what a beautiful song!

The words took me back to the days when Waikiki was the only thing I knew in the whole wide world. Kapiolani Park, picnickers, game-players, and joggers. Up ahead was the Ala Wai Canal. The old jungle was all but gone by this point, replaced by high rise apartments, hotels and restaurants. For some strange reason, I turned left off the Ala Wai and onto Royal Hawaiian Place. A large cement truck slowed down in front of me and a guy in a hard hat ran out in the street and held up his hand for me to stop. The truck driver began to back his big rig onto the construction site. Crash Kealoha announced, half-shouting, "It is now 11:15 Pacific Standard Time."

What did I do a stupid thing like turn onto Royal Hawaiian Place for? The morning's gone already. I gotta check the stands and get back to the shop!

I banged both my hands down on the steering wheel in exasperation. Cement began to pour through the funnel at the rear of the truck. I turned the radio up to blot out the grating noise.

"And now I've got a classic for you," the disc jockey cut in. "Don Ho and *It Ain't No Big Thing*." Don came on with his carefree manner, and the thought suddenly came to me that stewin' and worryin' get you no place. The past and future are all wrapped up in the right now. It's what you do with that now that counts. Simple! It ain't no big thing. Hell, I discovered that on the beach a long time ago, only I never realized until now how smart I was!

The flow of wet cement was shut off. The hard hat stepped back and whistled me forward.

"Howzit, brother?" I waved.

"Aw, we're lookin' good!" he yelled back.

"Aw right!"

At the end of the street, the sign said "Left Turn Only." I followed the curving arrows painted on the pavement in front of me and I was back on Kalakaua Avenue. It was a one way street by then, tall buildings lining both sides, and there were more going up. I likened myself at that moment to being at the bottom of a steep canyon, with two ways to go: follow the stream and hope you live long enough to see some daylight, or take a deep breath and start climbing for the top, no matter how steep and hazardous the ascent may be. I'd made it before and, by God, I could do it again. I knew just the place to start.

I pulled into the underground garage next to the Moana Hotel, walked out onto the avenue and into the first shop I could find.

"Can I help you?" the salesgirl asked.

"I wanna buy a pair of trunks like the ones over there."

"You know your size?"

"Two inches larger than the last time."

"Beg pardon, sir?" she said.

"Size 34," I replied.

"Napoleon! What're you doing around here?" It was the doorman at the Moana, with ten years added onto his face.

"I'm slummin' today," I replied, waving my small package at him.

"At the prices they get in here, you must be kiddin' me!"

I headed straight through the lobby for the men's room, stripped out of my clothes and into my new trunks. I rolled my shirt, shorts, pants and shoes into a ball, walked back out through the lobby to the garage. I threw the bundle into the trunk of my car and followed the rear exit out onto the beach.

The big hotels had done their job well. Every grain of sand in Waikiki was covered by a beach chair, a mat, a towel, or a body. The water was alive with people like ants on a plate of honey. LeRoy Ah Choi spotted me on the beachwalk and waved from the wet sand. Rabbit Kekai, his hair turned to gray and 30 pounds heavier, stared out to sea from behind the counter of a small beach stand. The Royal Hawaiian still looked the same, her sands gleaming white, protected from the treading masses by a linked chain of exclusivity.

Crossing on top of the sea wall on my way to the Halekulani and my first stand, I wondered if she would be there. The tide was high, temporarily robbing the tiny beach of some much-needed space. My heart jumped when I saw her, a picture of loveliness sunning on the sand.

"Good morning," I greeted her. "All recovered from the fights last night, I hope?"

"Uh, huh. I think so. Yes. But I don't think I'll go back for a while."

"Do you mind if I sit down and visit with you?" I asked.

"Please do. I'd like that."

We talked of many things, this beautiful girl and I. She had a witty charm and refinement about her that fascinated me right from the start. When I got up to leave, we made a dinner date for that evening.

I looked out at the ocean in front of the Reef Hotel. Alan Napoleon was swimming after one of our surfboards. What a blessing it was to have my two nephews, Alan and Maltby, working for me. Looking at them, I could see myself 25 years ago. They were the new breed at Waikiki now.

Maltby was behind the stand when I approached, and Alan had just seen his pupil safely ashore. They were both surprised to see me at this hour in a pair of trunks. I know they thought of me as Uncle Barry, the money man that solved the problems and paid the bills. No doubt I had come down to the stand to mix a little business with pleasure.

I unlocked the petty cash box and handed each of the two boys five dollars. "Here, you guys go have lunch. It's on me today."

"But who's going to watch the stand?" Maltby asked.

"Hey, what'd you think? I was raised on this beach," I said. "Now, get going, before I change my mind and you gotta buy your own lunch."

And there I was, back where only I knew I had to be. After what I'd been through and all the places I'd been, I knew it wouldn't be easy, picking up the scattered pieces to the once nearly-completed puzzle that was my life. But already I had made a good start. I was back on the beach that I loved. I had a date with a new young lady. My two nephews, expert watermen, were with me. And where our paths would lead, only time could tell. After all, the name of the game is try, and as my old pal, Chubby Mitchell, used to say, "If can, can. If no can, no can."

"Hey, mister. Would you like to rent a surfboard?"

Epilogue

He's as at home in the water as he is on shore. He's a babysitter, a qualified life guard, a policeman, a teacher, a companion, a friend and, yes, sometimes even a lover. The beach is his life, and Waikiki is his home.

Just who are these guys who become beachboys? Where are they from? They are of predominantly Hawaiian extraction, raised on the beach—or lived close enough by to wake up each morning to the smells and sounds of the sea.

Why, in this day and age, would anyone want to make a career of being a beachboy? The money can't be all that great and with the wages labor demands today, surely he could find a more lucrative field!

Money has nothing to do with it. He loves the water, good times, social contact, and freedom. He has witnessed the steady demise of a people and their ways, caught up in a world not of their making. Physically, he is big enough and strong enough to fight for the things that he feels are his by natural lineage. In so doing, he had at times run afoul of the rules and authorities who have deemed it their business to stand in his way. Thus, maybe

90 percent of the beach boys, starting with the early fifties, have police records of one sort or another—minor infractions for the most part, but black marks just the same. These same black marks have been used by these self-proclaimed "authorities" to gain control of the beach by allowing them determine who can and who can't work.

But these people—these "authorities"—they come and go. Their heart is in something else. But The Keepers of the Sand will always remain.

Acknowledgements

Barry would like to extend a very warm thank you to the following people who supported this book's publication through Kickstarter:

Amanda Hermanson
Naomi L. Medieros
Jo Kahuanui
Nancy Emerson
Frank Weight
Leslie Hoxie Thornton
Rebekka Stone
Valentina Tondaleiya Lopez-Cannon

www.ingramcontent.com/pod-product-compliance
Lightning Source LLC
Chambersburg PA
CBHW032026290426
44110CB00012B/694